God's blessings!

Jerri Olson

# Spending Time with God

## THE ART OF CHRISTIAN MEDITATION AND PRAYER

TAMERA THORESON

WESTBOW
PRESS®
A DIVISION OF THOMAS NELSON
& ZONDERVAN

WestBow Press books may be ordered through booksellers or by contacting:

WestBow Press
A Division of Thomas Nelson & Zondervan
1663 Liberty Drive
Bloomington, IN 47403
www.westbowpress.com
844-714-3454

ISBN: 978-1-6642-4109-1 (sc)
ISBN: 978-1-6642-4110-7 (hc)
ISBN: 978-1-6642-4108-4 (e)

Library of Congress Control Number: 2021914657

Print information available on the last page.

WestBow Press rev. date: 08/13/2021

May these words of my mouth and this meditation of my heart be pleasing in your sight, Lord, my Rock and my Redeemer.

—Psalm 19:14 (NIV)

To my mother, Veronica, whose example of praying and trusting God with her life was an inspiration to everyone who knew her. She was on her knees every night and prayed all nine of us kids through thick and thin. Her kind personality made it seem easy to forgive all the free-spirited things her children did, but I think she was always seeing the good in everyone. Her last comment to me before she passed into Jesus's loving arms was this: "You were all good kids." When I think about her initial desire to become a nun, which is such an opposite extreme from having nine children, I am so glad she decided having a family was her calling. Nevertheless, God was always her first love—and her spirit runs deep in this book. Thank you, Mom, for teaching us to pray.

# Contents

# Introduction

Welcome to *Spending Time with God: The Art of Christian Meditation and Prayer.*

My prayer and meditation time has become my favorite part of the day. This routine, where I put my Creator first in my life, has given me a sense of stability and wisdom that was missing before. It is a time where I can feel true joy, be totally myself, open up to a higher being, and feel secure, energized, and loved beyond what the world can give me. This experience is open to anyone who is longing for a deeper relationship with their higher power or wants to strengthen their faith.

Many of the big decisions and inspirations of my life have come out of things the Holy Spirit has put on my heart during this time. As I have been spending devoted time with Jesus, my relationship has grown into a rich, complex, and fulfilling experience. I have been inspired to do things that I am totally unprepared to do, but somehow people come into my life—and everything falls into place.

When sharing my experiences with people about this, so many say they struggle with finding the time or place to pray and meditate. A calling developed in my heart to try to explore solutions to these struggles, and that is what inspired me to write this book. It's not that people don't want to spend time with God, there are a multitude of reasons why it isn't happening for them. By exploring possible reasons and setting yourself up for success, you can have a deep relationship with Him, which will be the most important thing you do all day.

Personally, it has not always been easy to connect with my Creator. I was raised in a Christian family, and even though I didn't consider my faith to be strong as a youth and teen, I always knew God was there. Looking back, I can see how His power permeated my life.

One of the struggles I had as a youth was that I viewed God just as an authority figure who watched everything I did, judged it, and then punished me or expected me to pay penance if I was not perfect. It was difficult to call Him my friend; subsequently, I did not want to invest in a relationship with Him. I remember times when I was about ten or eleven, where I felt intense fear and feeling like something intangible was there, especially at night, but I didn't know that I could call on the name of Jesus. If anyone is experiencing anything like this at night, I want you to know the name of Jesus has the power to remove darkness.

In my high school years, like so many teens, I was very vulnerable because I did not have a strong sense of who I was spiritually—and I did not know what God could do. As I grew older and read the Bible for myself, my views changed to more of a loving God who sent His Son to save me, who is above me, but mostly beside me. He is always helping and eagerly forgiving me when I ask.

God put needed people into my life to inspire me to learn more about Him, including my church family, my biological family, and my Bible study friends. As my faith journey went on, I discovered prayer time to be healing, inspiring, and powerful.

Prayer and meditation may be a totally new concept to you—or maybe you are just curious about learning more. Regardless, I hope that by sharing ideas and experiences, all can benefit and grow deeper in our faith.

Whether you are a CEO or a student, you can benefit from carving this time out of your day:

> I will instruct you and teach you in the way you
> should go. I will counsel you with my loving eye
> on you. (Psalm 32:8)

The wisest people seek counsel from the Lord. Historically, American presidents have sought counsel from spiritual leaders to help them gain wisdom. Going through life without Jesus and trying to figure everything out by yourself is like living life by a dim light. It is like using a matchstick for light when you have the sun.

> In him was life, and that life was the light of all
> mankind. The light shines in the darkness, and
> the darkness has not overcome. (John 1:4–5)

# 1

# God Is Always Teaching Us through His Word and People

From the day we are born to the day we leave this world, we are changing and learning. Through scripture, God tells us that He has His loving eye on us and that He is instructing and teaching us. He does this through a combination of His Word and our interactions with other people.

The obvious people who teach us are those who have chosen to give their lives to preaching the Gospel as a career: pastors. Less obvious are those we come into contact with at work or within our families.

When we grow impatient with someone or have a conflict, may we consider them to be a teacher? We can use these situations to initiate new ways of responding and new ways of treating others, as Jesus would have. They have a gift for us, a learning opportunity presented as a struggle. They can learn from us as well as we show gentleness, kindness, humility/humbleness, and forgiveness. However, we cannot solve these problems without help from the Father. Therefore, by staying in contact with Him and letting Him counsel us in our relationships through the Word and time with Him, we will have strong bonds that cannot easily be broken.

It was suggested to me by more than one person that I should share some of my lifetime struggles and how God has helped me. Some of this is very personal and feels like baring my soul, but God has given me the courage to share it so that possibly someone's life will be helped and changed. I want so much for everyone to have the love of God in their hearts, but I know that this is not realistic. If even one person makes the commitment to carve time out of his or her day to spend with Jesus, it will be worth it.

I grew up the youngest of nine children on a farm in the Midwest. Needless to say, the world did not revolve around me. I have generally happy memories of my childhood, but I was very introverted and struggled with self-esteem. I would hide behind my mom whenever anyone would try to talk to me. Speaking up or sharing my opinion was never comfortable for me. I was kind of in survival mode, and when new opportunities came up, fear always won. I did not see myself as a leader or ever having anything of worth to share with the world. It is only through the act of spending time with Jesus and receiving the transforming energy that I have been able to go beyond my fears and take on challenges. I was able to get beyond my insecurities because God had a plan for me—using a small, insignificant person to do things I never could have done on my own.

My parents did the best they could with so many children, which was somewhat normal back in the 1970s. My dad was a farmer, and we always had food on the table. My memories of my dad are very different than my oldest siblings' memories because they remember a family man, but I remember how my parents' relationship suffered to the point where they divorced soon after I graduated from high school and left the house. My father allowed himself to be distracted by things other than his wife and family, and this left wounds on those of us still in the home at the time.

Anyone who has been in a home where divorce is near can tell you that the environment can be extremely difficult. Typically, the adults are consumed with their own problems and are operating on cruise control. That is one of the reasons why when I started spending time with God, I finally felt fully loved. He can soothe the injured parts of your heart and mind so that you can be healed and whole.

Every parent makes mistakes, and through the process of forgiveness, I am learning ways to honor my dad by listening to people tell stories about him in the early years, people who knew him differently. God helped me forgive him by trying to see the situation through his eyes. For example, the fact that he waited to leave until after all the children graduated was a sacrifice on his part for the entire family's sake. He was very unhappy in the marriage, but he remained in it because of us children. Even though it was more painful for me to endure their unraveling relationship, and I was actually relieved when my sister told me they divorced, he most likely thought it would be more painful for us to live through their divorce during high school in a small town.

Unfortunately, my dad passed away when I was twenty-five, and I never really got to talk this through with him. Lesson learned: people who do things that appear to be the worst may have underlying good intentions. It's not that we can never feel angry about things that happened or get mad at someone for making poor decisions; it's that we can try to see their perspective and have empathy even for those who hurt us. God can give you the ability to forgive and heal big wounds if you allow Him into your heart and mind.

Having a Christian role model in my mom was huge as I look back. She was a hard worker around the house, and her faith was very important to her. Every day, she would get on her knees and pray for us children because she knew she couldn't do everything she wanted to do for us; she needed Jesus to fill the gaps. With a kind, humble spirit, she performed all the duties of a homemaker and was "Jesus with skin on." She once told me that she knew I was going to be all right because she asked God to watch over us. What a woman of faith!

My siblings also played a huge role in my life at different

times. By encouraging me to go to college, being prayer warriors, mentors, and friends, witnessing to me about their faith, or showing how to put their faith first, each of them has had influence. Don't get me wrong; none of us are perfect, and we had our issues. If you ever watched the movie *Little Women*, there are some similarities to our family. But the other big things in my life would not have happened had my siblings not been there when others were telling me I didn't need to go to college or that it was not OK to seek out my own faith.

Who are the people in your life who have influenced your faith?

_____

_____

_____

Life struggles are sometimes a plan that God has to lead you to another person or place. As a teen, I had some very negative experiences with dating, and I was determined not to ever date again. But God had a plan for me, and in college, I met my husband who had had one similar experience in his dating life. He was one of the first people who spoke to me of a loving God who we can talk to and who can take away our worries. He wanted the same things as I did, had Christian values, and was respectful of me, so we were married three years later. Marrying my wonderful husband and having our four beautiful children were all answers to prayers that went beyond my expectations.

When my children were little, it was a huge struggle to find time to read the Bible or pray. So, if you are in this time of your life, I empathize. But you can find time, and you need to find time. This is the most important thing you do all day, and your children need you to be a good example. More on how to do this later!

God has always been leading and guiding me. When I went back to college for a master's degree in education, I was given the inspiration and determination to write a handwriting curriculum that coordinates with reading programs called ezWrite. When I thought about this project initially, it felt like I was climbing Mount Everest. I prayed for direction and a way to open a path for this new journey. He connected me with a Christian person, Mary Beckman, who also was passionate about this subject, and we worked together to create a program that we both know was God's work in us. This curriculum has been such a blessing to many and continues to grow across the US and Canada.

Another calling came when I was home for six weeks recovering from surgery. I felt a very strong pull to start a homeless shelter program in our area. Again, God connected me with another person, Barb Wisnewski, who also had a passion for the homeless. We started meeting, inviting others, and found out that God was calling many people in our community to this mission. Currently, there is a program called Great River Family Promise that helps families get back on their feet by finding them jobs and housing, and there has been very little recurrence of homelessness.

God is continually directing my life and giving me courage to move forward with goals that seem impossible or beyond my abilities. He has sent my husband and me on mission trips to places we initially feared or had no interest in (but then fell in love with), including Africa, Costa Rica, and Alaska, and places in our own city and country. We asked Him to help us have the funds to do this and set up an account, putting a little bit away from each paycheck. It's amazing to see how this grows and how we are blessed when we give to something beyond ourselves.

There is no question to me that God is listening and answering prayers. How could someone with such a low self-esteem, who did not want a relationship, and did not see themselves as able to contribute to the world, have these opportunities and the courage to pursue them? Only by the grace of God.

When you pray and meditate on God's Word, a cycle of empowerment and success emerges. You will have peace that goes beyond human understanding. You may be called and given skills that you never knew were available. God can use you to do things you never dreamed possible if you spend time with Him and let Him lead and guide you.

Just as we were all created uniquely, there are different ways in which we can share time with God. In our busy lives, many of us struggle with finding the time and space to do this. In the past, I would have all the good intentions of reading the Bible or a devotion, and one thing after another kept distracting me until all the time I had set aside was gone.

The purpose of this book is to explore how we can create a time and place to do what I believe it the most important thing we do all day. So many people I talk to struggle with this, and that is my motivation for this book: to help others develop a strong relationship with Jesus, resulting peace and prosperity. So, grab yourself a cup of coffee or tea, and let's do this together!

Write about your faith story. How have events in your life shaped where you are with your faith right now? How are you feeling about your prayer time? What are your struggles and hopes for this journey?

_____

_____

_____

_____

_____

Prayer: Heavenly Father, I open my eyes, heart, and mind to this process. I want to learn the art of prayer and meditation so that I can grow in my faith. Please help me draw from Your strength and develop this new skill so I can know and love You more each day. Amen.

# 2

# What Is Meditation and Prayer Time?

Meditation has changed and morphed so much over the past century. There are so many ways to meditate today that this activity has no specific definition anymore. For me, the word *meditation* used to conjure up a picture of someone sitting cross-legged on the floor and chanting. While this specific practice may be important to other religions, meditation can look different according to the Bible.

Christians are encouraged to meditate on scripture, but there are no rules for how you should sit or what you should say. There are references to kneeling, standing, sitting, laying prostrate, holding hands out, bowing down, and looking up for different situations. Therefore, there is freedom to make choices about how this looks for each individual. Some people need something visual to focus on, and some need to close their eyes to focus. Some people repeat a verse or a specific thought, such as gratitude, and some people concentrate on their breathing and picture God as a being. You can picture God's hands open to you, accepting all your problems, thankfulness, and praise, or His loving arms around you.

God wants you to have a relationship with Him. Since He created us all uniquely, the way you interact with Him is going to be different and special. He has a plan for you that includes exciting adventures infused with helping people who are waiting for you to answer God's call. The longer you wait to do this, the longer those people will not have you doing what you were born to do.

If you feel you need specific direction in this particular way, I encourage you to look up the Bible verses about prayer and meditation listed below. The Bible is our guide for every area of our lives.

So, what is meditation anyway? Meditation has many different forms and is not specific to Christian teachings. Meditation, from a Christian perspective, focuses on God and His Word. Based on my studies and experiences with it, I believe it is a practice where an individual offers a sacrifice of quiet time to focus their mind on their Creator, scripture, or inspired ideas. It is used to develop the relationship and communication with the Creator.

Meditation teaches us how to live, and it can be used to give peace and rest to achieve a mentally clear and emotionally calm state, to reduce stress, anxiety, and pain, and to increase mental peace, creativity, energy, prosperity, and well-being. It can open the mind to new ideas, provide direction to take action, or provide help giving forgiveness by softening the heart and giving the courage to apologize.

Meditation increases the depth of our relationships with our Creator because of the sacrifice of time, and it can be used as a form of worship:

> Keep this Book of the Law always on your lips; meditate on it day and night, so that you may be careful to do everything written in it. Then you will be prosperous and successful. (Joshua 1:8)

> I meditate on your precepts and consider your ways. (Psalm 119:15)

But his delight is in the law of the Lord, and on his law, he meditates day and night. (Psalm 1:2)

I lift up my hands to your commands, which I love, and I meditate on your decrees. (Psalm 119:48)

I will meditate on all your works and consider all your mighty deeds. (Psalm 77:12)

My eyes stay open through the watches of the night, that I may meditate on your promises. (Psalm 119:148)

There are a lot of scripture versus about meditation! In essence, we are to meditate on the commandments, on His Word, on God, on the teachings, on the ways of the Lord, on the good things He has done for us, and on what He is going to do in the future.

Other verses refer to "being still," and Zechariah 2:13 and Psalm 46:10 tell us to make time to rest in His presence. Although we don't know why meditation is not part of every Christian's routine, we can start to make it part of ours, so that we can reap the benefits of this ancient yet lasting discipline.

Growing up, we always went to church and recited prayers before meals and bedtime. But the first time I can truly remember being still before the Lord and getting an "answer" was when I was in college. I was struggling because I had initially thought I wanted to be an accountant. My high school accounting teacher, Mr. Olson, made it very interesting and engaging.

As I went through the college accounting classes, the reality that I did not want to spend my life doing accounting work hit me. I felt lost and confused. I cried, wanted to quit school, and was desperate to find another career.

I sat alone in my college apartment, wondering what I was

going to do, and I prayed for an answer. It came during a career exploration class where the words "occupational therapy" captured my attention like a blinking neon sign. I had very little experience with people with disabilities or occupational therapy (OT), but as I explored this career, I found out that it was the perfect fit.

Being born with a high level of empathy toward people who are struggling, there are times where I believe I actually feel some of their pain, as strange as that may sound.

There are memories during my school years where I would be caught thinking about a student who was struggling. For example, there were students with disabilities—such as one with alopecia (a disorder where you lose all your hair) and another who probably had an autism type disorder—who were always alone. The teacher would call my name, and I would not have heard what the lesson was. Their pain was sinking into me and reverberating in my mind like a movie scene that kept replaying in my head. I would want to engage them on the playground, but I was introverted and could not overcome my own weaknesses.

The thought of learning how to be comfortable with students with disabilities and living my life working with these angels on earth made my heart sing. Now, after over thirty years in the field of OT, it is undeniable that this was an answer to prayer from God. Am I still an introvert? Yes, but God has filled the gaps so that I can be brave when Tamera would prefer to stay home. I can honestly say that there has not been a day that I have wished I had not gone to work. I work with the most disabled children in our schools. They have physical and emotional issues, so it is hard work, but it is rewarding and definitely what God intended for me to do. I am so glad that I looked to Him to help me make this career choice.

There is only One who knows you inside and out, and that is your Creator. He wants to be your friend and confidant. If you submit your heart to Him, He will lead and guide you as you spend time with Him.

What Is Prayer?

Prayer, by definition, is a communication to a higher power (God) through thought, word, or song. Prayer is done by those who trust that they are heard by the power of a higher being. It can be used as praise or to ask for help, wisdom, or forgiveness. It can be done as an individual or as part of a group.

This book focuses mainly on individual prayer, but we will briefly explore verses about praying together since this is important too. According to scripture, the intention of your prayer is everything:

> And when you pray, do not be like the hypocrites, for they love to pray standing in the synagogues and on the street corners, to be seen by men. (Matthew 6:5)

In biblical times, there were people who were adamant about following rules, and they thought that was the way to salvation. However, it ended up being more of a show for people than truly what God wanted them to be doing.

God wants us to pray, but our prayer time needs to be for God and our relationship with Him—and not to show others how holy we are or for recognition. When we gather in His name, He will be with us. We can focus on Him, the Author and Perfecter of our faith.

Both alone prayer time and gathering together to pray are important for your faith walk:

> They all joined together constantly in prayer, along with the women and Mary, the mother of Jesus, and with his brothers. (Acts 1:14)

Scripture makes it clear that prayer together is a staple activity for a healthy faith life. It is not *if* we pray, but *when* we pray, all the time, in every situation.

Praying together in worship, at mealtimes, and at bedtime was always a regular, very comfortable routine for me, because my mom established them from as early as I can remember. Every night we would say, "Dear Jesus, I love you. Dear Jesus, I want you. Dear Jesus, come into my heart." We would recite all the names of my family and my eight siblings: "God bless Mama, Daddy, Bobby, Judy, Bruce, Rita, Val, Sharon, Janice, Irene, and Tammy and make me a good little girl, amen."

That routine got so ingrained that I always went to sleep after saying a prayer. But praying alone and meditating was a very foreign concept. I actually thought it was a little weird for someone to go into a room, close the door, and sit in total quiet. For what? I was too busy for that. It sounded boring, and quite frankly, I thought my life was going just fine without it. That's exactly where many people are mentally. They don't need Jesus in their lives because they are trying to do it themselves. Our culture looks down on needing help, and it admires independence, which can be good—or is it?

Working hard and earning an income to support your family is good and actually biblical:

> Anyone who does not provide for their relatives, and especially for their own household, has denied the faith and is worse than an unbeliever. (1 Timothy 5:8)

> Thus says the Lord: "Cursed is the one who trusts in man, who draws strength from mere flesh and whose heart turns away from the Lord." (Jeremiah 17:5)

We are not supposed to do life alone and independent of our Creator. We can be both independent providers for our families *and* submissive to our Creator, our Advocate, and our Leader.

By worshipping and praying with others, we can have human and spiritual guides for our lives. I'm quite sure God was always calling me, but I was not listening. I let the world keep me busy and just content enough to not need Him. Little did I know, I was missing out on the best relationship I could ever have and laying a foundation for emotional, spiritual, and physical health.

When I left my hometown, where I had made many mistakes, it was a new beginning for me. I was able to present myself however I wanted to. No one knew who I had been, which was scary but very freeing.

Then there was a new beginning when my husband and I joined a church family. We made new friends and could share our love of Christ without holding back like we had to do with some of our friends who were not Christians. While there are many good people out there who you can and should be friends with, and it's important to reach out to non-Christians, we need to realize that who we spend time with does have an influence on us. You become like those with whom you spend time. Opening your friendship circle to Christian friends who you admire and pursuing their friendship will enrich your life. My husband and I have seen the power of having people pray for us many times over.

Jesus hung out with nonbelievers, but who He really had deep relationships with were His disciples because He could share His faith with them. They prayed with Him, and they were with him in good times and bad, for weddings and deaths.

Praying alone is also biblically based. Here are some verses— and you could probably find a lot more:

> Do not be anxious about anything, but in
> every situation, by prayer and petition, with

thanksgiving, present your requests to God. And the peace of God, which transcends all understanding, will guard your hearts and your minds in Christ Jesus. (Philippians 4:6–7)

But when you pray, go into your room, close the door and pray to your Father, who is unseen. Then your Father, who sees what is done in secret, will reward you. And when you pray, do not keep on babbling like pagans, for they think they will be heard because of their many words. Do not be like them, for your Father know what you need before you ask Him. (Matthew 6:6–8)

After he had dismissed them, He went up on a mountainside by Himself to pray. (Matthew 14:23)

After leaving them, He went up on a mountainside to pray. (Mark 6:46)

One of those days, Jesus went out to a mountainside to pray, and spent the night praying to God. (Luke 6:12)

In the early morning while it was still dark, Jesus got up, left the house, and went away to a secluded place, and was praying there. (Mark 1:35)

But Jesus Himself would often slip away to the wilderness and pray. (Luke 9:18)

There is no denying that the verses suggest that you need a quiet space to get away and be alone and take a chunk of time to just be with Jesus.

If you are a beginner with prayer and meditation, pick one of these verses that resonates with you and repeat it slowly three times. Pause between each time you read it for as long as is comfortable to allow your mind to process. This is one way for beginners to learn the art of prayer and meditation. You have just taken the initial step to meditation!

When I read scripture, the words feel like they are sinking into the deepest parts of my mind, body, and soul. Like medicine, I feel changed on a cellular level for the better. These changes are progress toward the new self that God has established in motion right now. Many people in the Bible, from Abram to Saul, were given new names as they started their new lives in Jesus. They were given a fresh start, and by enlisting the power of the Holy Spirit, they could now live a life with meaning—a transformed life.

1.  What types of meditation have you tried?

   _____

   _____

   _____

2.  Is meditating easy or hard for you and why?

   _____

   _____

   _____

3. Did repeating the verse above help you focus on it?

_____

_____

_____

4. Do you prefer to pray alone or with others?

_____

_____

_____

Prayer: Heavenly Father, thank You for helping me learn about prayer and meditation and how You created me to have a unique relationship with You. Though this process, I am taking steps toward knowing You more each day. I look forward to a rich relationship and life with You. Amen.

# 3

# Why Do We Meditate and Pray?

Everyone needs a positive way to start the day. We need a best friend who will never leave us, someone who can help us release fear and anxiety and give us confidence, strength, healing, and love.

In our marriage, there are mostly good times, but there are also times where there is frustration. My husband is a wonderful guy. But sometimes I expect my husband to do what I want or fulfill emotional needs when he is not ready or able. No one in my life, not even my husband, can or should take on all of these things for me. I have a lot of "stuff," but Jesus wants it all! He *wants* us to come to Him with our problems, needs, and desires of our hearts. Many times, I come home from work, having been traumatized by the situations my students have endured. Many of the children have been neglected or abused or have progressive diseases and are slowly dying. I have been attacked physically and emotionally. I can sense when my husband has shut down. Every child is different and has unique problems in special education, and every year, we encounter even more severe things. Who can I go to when I have maxed out my husband? The Father.

God answers all prayers. He rejoices when we bring to Him the problems He already knows about. He can lead and guide us through the dusty roads of adversity and the tangled messes we encounter or create. When we have fiery words, He can calm our tongues. If we have resentment, He can soften our hearts, allowing forgiveness to melt in. When we need new and fresh ideas, He has the answers. When we pray, we enlist the power of the Holy Spirit to inspire us to take action and solve problems.

Giving God our problems doesn't mean we are giving up or are being weak. It is being wise enough to know there is a higher power who is our Healer and Helper. A real-life example of an answered prayer was when my husband, Eric, and I went on a trip to wine country and started becoming infatuated with wine. We started having a glass of wine every night and then two glasses. We knew it was starting to get out of control, and we prayed about it.

Around that time, Eric had a virtual doctor's appointment to discuss his medications, and the doctor asked us about alcohol. He asked us to stop drinking, and we initially felt defensive, but looking back, I know it was an answer to prayer. We needed that person to give us a reality check and prevent us from sliding dangerously down a road we did not want to go on.

Giving this problem to God during prayer time helped fill the gap between the problem and our human abilities. Could we have made that decision on our own? Possibly. But we choose to entrust our lives to God who has power beyond human ability. Having gone through that experience really has made our relationship stronger.

We have choices to make with our lives and our time every day, and the world is so full of opportunities to engage in negativity. The television news takes scenes out of context, making them seem more dramatic to engage our emotions. This is a marketing tool to get you hooked on that emotional response that gets you "going" in the morning.

This repeated exposure takes a toll because it evokes emotions of fear and anxiety. This anxiety, small as it may seem, triggers neurochemicals in your brain, and repeated exposure to this does change your mental state. The charge of energy you feel when watching it can be so addicting that the next morning, you want to repeat that feeling. Every morning, you are bathing your brain in stress hormones that change how you think and behave. Be careful what you put into your brain every day.

The radio can also be another source of negativity, and spending every morning listening to negative content can create a negative trajectory for your day. Announcers have become masters at saying more and more outrageous things to sustain your attention and keep you coming back for more. They have vulgar contests that people become absorbed in during their commutes to work. It is easy to become entrapped by the shock and awe of someone having an affair; their stories can be dramatic and more exciting than our own lives.

Thank goodness we have choices. When you start your day in a positive way by spending time with the God of hope, He fills you with joy and peace rather than negativity. If you don't want to do your prayer and meditation at this time, you can listen to positive music, read positive material, pray with your kids and spouse, go for a walk and observe nature, or call someone and tell them you are thinking of them. By starting the day with positivity, you can put your trust in Him all day long, knowing that He is with you and preparing the way for you.

Who does not want to be overflowing with hope by the power of the Holy Spirit? Loving the Lord your God with all your heart and all your soul and with all your mind is the greatest commandment (Matthew 22). He wants a relationship with you, and He wants to spend time with you.

If you want your plans to succeed, commit them to the Lord during this time of prayer, and He will work out everything in His time and in ways that will surpass anything you could do on your own.

Jobs can be a blessing or huge source of frustration, and almost everyone has been ready to leave their jobs at one point or another. When I prayed for my husband when he was struggling with his job, and then was laid off, we were in one of the most difficult times of our marriage. It was uncomfortable because we typically did not pray together, but after that first awkward time, it became such a blessing for us to give our worries to God. He answered our prayers, and my husband was offered a new job that fit his work style better, and bonus, he gets paid way better! What seemed like a curse, God turned into a huge blessing both in our relationship and with my husband's career.

When you spend time with God, He will restore your soul, comfort you in times of trouble, and give you the words you need to hear and the actions you should take.

You do not need to worry. If you cast your burdens on Him, He will provide exactly what you need. (Psalm 55:22) If we fix our eyes on Jesus, we will not grow weary or lose heart.

God also uses illness and hard times for good. When I was at home for six weeks recovering from surgery, I was in the middle of a Bible study called "Jesus the One and Only" by Beth Moore. Having to stay home, I had more time to devote to the Bible study and meditate on the message. What became clear to me was a call to help the homeless in our community. Right before the surgery, I had been working with a small group at one of the elementary schools, and one of the activities I wanted the students to do was draw a picture of their house. One of the students just sat and did nothing, and when I questioned Him, he told me he did not have a house. They lived in a car. I felt horrible for having brought this reality forward, and the sadness overwhelmed me.

This started a conversation with our social worker that piqued my interest in helping homeless families. Through research, I found out that every time a student changes schools, which happens frequently with homeless students, they lose months of learning. I also learned that our area did not have an option for homeless families to stay in the community; they had to move to another county for shelter, which meant switching schools, and the parents struggled to find jobs because they did not have any connections in the community. The realities of homelessness in our community were becoming clearer to me every day, and God kept nudging me to delve into this problem.

During my meditation time, God put a goal in my heart to help families who are struggling with homelessness stay in their communities and find jobs and housing. He helped me find other people who were passionate about this to join together as a mission team. He paved the path to finding other churches that would join us. It was a huge undertaking, but now, Great River Family Promise (GRFP) has been helping families in the surrounding communities overcome homelessness. They have very few families go back to homelessness once they have been helped because they solve the underlying issues. God uses many adverse situations to create something new. Many of the people who have experienced homelessness and have been in the GRFP program go on to help others in need. Had I not had that surgery and time to sit and reflect on His Word, I would have never had the opportunity to help start this ministry.

Meditating on God's commandments make us wise, and His Word is a light that shows us the way for our lives. You will find He has the most wonderful sense of humor and creativity. Your prayers will be answered, many times in surprising and unexpected ways.

Of course, this is not a magic wand that creates a utopia where there are no problems. You will have trouble in this life, but God wants you to bring those things to Him. We were not meant to do everything on our own; He created us to need Him and to go to Him for every need (see Romans 15:13; Matthew 22:37; Proverbs 16:3; Psalm 23:2–3; Hebrews 12:2; Psalm 119:148; 119:97–99, 46:1; Deuteronomy 6:5).

1. Why is it important to pray and meditate?

_____

_____

_____

2. How does the idea of giving your problems to God feel to you?

_____

_____

_____

3. Are you able to recognize negativity on the TV or radio and change the channel?

_____

_____

_____

4. What are some options for positive TV and radio?

_____

_____

_____

5. Have you ever witnessed a bad situation used for good?

_____

_____

_____

Prayer: Heavenly Father, thank You for Your open invitation to share time with You and for being the One who is always there for us. You allow us to come into Your presence to share our worries, fears, hopes, and dreams. Help us make good decisions about how we spend our time and inspire us to focus our energy on the direction You have chosen for our lives. Amen.

# 4

# Setting Up Your Space for Success

Creating a space that promotes the right frame of mind and openness to communication with God can make all the difference in your experience. Matthew 14:23 and Luke 6:12 tell us that Jesus would go to the mountain to pray.

It would be great if we all had a real mountain in our backyards to go up to when we want to share time and space with God, but the reality is that most of us live in cities and not near mountains.

In those days, people lived in very small homes, and Jesus probably did not have a quiet space to separate Himself from the rest of the family. Considering His situation, He needed guaranteed uninterrupted time. I believe that the point of this scripture is that Jesus knew He needed a quiet space to connect with God—away from all the distractions. He needed time with His Father.

Our homes are abuzz with activity. TVs, computers, phones, children, pets, and significant others are great, but they compete for our time and attention:

> So we fix our eyes not on what is seen, but on what is unseen, since what is seen is temporary, but what is unseen is eternal. (2 Corinthians 4:18)

You need to create a buffer zone of silence around you in order to focus on unseen things; otherwise, your senses will automatically shift your awareness away to the sounds and sights that dominate our attention.

It is way easier to focus on the world and all the distractions, and the natural world does reflect God's glory. However, if you are outside watching boats go by, or if your quiet time is in your car on your way to work, you might want to evaluate if that is truly a source of quiet and meditation. I'm not saying the car isn't a good time to listen to Christian music or pray—we should pray all the time—but in the space you have chosen, can you reflect on a scripture verse, listen to what God is saying to you, and possibly write it down for future reference? Are you truly devoting time to Him, or are you multitasking and combining this with something else you have to do or want to do?

Based on scripture verses of how Jesus went away to a quiet place, I believe your best option for truly connecting with your Creator is creating a buffer zone of silence with no multitasking and no visual distractions. Learning this skill may be a bit of a struggle if you are not used to shutting out the world.

This does not mean that we have to be bored during this time. God is trying to transform you, and He sometimes helps your mind create new ideas, solve problems, and think differently. It may not be wrong if your mind starts to think about new things. If you need your mind to settle, God will help you settle it.

As you start to train your mind, a natural rhythm should start to occur. One of my friends tried to meditate, and she said, "I just can't do it." When I asked about it, I found out she dove in to try to sit in perfect quiet for twenty minutes, and she felt like a failure when she couldn't keep her mind on one thought for the whole time.

Start small and build on this time gradually as you are comfortable. This time—and the results of it—are all unique to you and God. This rich, inspiring time is all part of your blessed and inspired life. Your blessings will spill over into the lives all around you.

How do we shut out all these things and create a space that is open to the divine relationship we so desperately need? We have to be proactive to make this happen:

> But when you pray, go into your room, close the door and pray to your Father, who is unseen. Then your Father, who sees what is done in secret, will reward you. (Matthew 6:6)

So, let's start with *where*. Where is the one space that you could most likely get some alone time? It could be in an office, a bedroom, a closet, an attic, or a garage. Before you do anything to this space, take some time to think about the space and how it would function as your new meditation and prayer space.

Ask yourself some questions: Is the temperature going to remain in a comfortable range for you? Is the lighting or potential lighting adequate? Is there room for a chair, a cushion, or comfortable seating? Do you feel hopeful or see good potential about using this space for this purpose? Are you comfortable praying in this space the way it is—or would some simple changes help you focus?

Some people are able to do meditation in any place as long as they have their carpet square. I admire this ability, but I am not that person! Initially, I had an office space and the things I thought I needed, but I would get distracted so easily. My phone would beep, and my mind would wander. I would catch myself getting up and walking out of the room without even making the conscious decision to be done with my meditation time. *Wait a minute. I wasn't done yet. I'm supposed to be meditating. Sit back down!*

I was not able to focus without making some changes to the office space we had. It was too much like a traditional office, but I added a few inexpensive items to make it cozier and more peaceful. For me, I think the candle was the ticket. Lighting the candle signaled a starting point and cast a warm, calming glow in the room. I tend to have a racing mind, and the candle helped me settle in a little more mentally.

I also tried sitting at the dining room table, but it felt awkward because it was a place where others might walk by at any moment. I wasn't really comfortable holding my hands out, bowing my head, praying out loud, or letting my true self come forward when I was potentially being watched. It felt like I was studying for a college class more than connecting with a higher being.

Some people have said they can't focus completely on God when others are around, and I agree. Some days, someone would come in to make breakfast, turn on the TV, or try to talk to me about the upcoming day. They were just living a normal life, but I was starting to get irritated because of the distractions. I had to really look at what the problem was, and it was *me* because I didn't set myself up for success. I didn't find a place with potential for silence.

Next, gather the items you need so that when you have time for prayer, you don't waste a lot of time moving your furniture and supplies around. You will need:

- comfortable seating
- a small table or writing surface (lap table)
- lamp (if room lighting is insufficient)
- a Bible
- a good devotional (and a concordance if you would like to look up words in scripture)
- a journal
- pen and scratch paper

You can also add items that provide a calming environment, such as a candle, a plant or flowers, essential oils, inspiring pictures, or wall hangings.

I don't believe that God really cares what your room looks like. He will meet with you wherever you invite Him in. However, if you feel a certain color, such as green, which connects with nature, will help you be more open to communication with God, then by all means, get out your paint roller.

What you don't need during this time are visual distractions such as a TV, radio, computer, phone, or other electronic devices unless that is what you read your Bible or devotional on. If you can find a paper copy of a devotional, I find that it helps me to not get sidetracked into checking social media, email, or things that pop up on your phone or computer. One tip that has been helpful is to turn off your notifications or banners in all social media accounts so that you can check them when you want to and not when *they* want you to. If you travel, a devotional on an e-reader might be a good option since there tend to be fewer things popping up on your phone.

The goal of this part of your journey is to find a space that will create the best opportunity to connect with your Creator. Pray about this to Him. You can ask Him to bless the space and be present with you. Here is an example: "Dear heavenly Father, I ask You to help me find a quiet space to connect with You. I want to share time with You to develop a deeper relationship with You, and I need to find a space that we can be alone. Please bless this space and help me to honor You by taking part of my day and giving it to You. I invite You to be here with me every day while I read and meditate on Your Word."

Preparing your space to pray and meditate gives a sense of commitment, which is important for this process. Put all the things you need in place so that when your time comes, you don't have to look around for your things. You can be calm and hopeful in your new space.

Potential places:

_____

_____

_____

What items do I have?

_____

_____

_____

What items do I need?

_____

_____

_____

Prayer: Heavenly Father, help me find a place where I can spend undistracted time with You. Give me peace, joy, and hope as I try to develop the skills of prayer and meditation. I know that there will be trials and setbacks, but You are with me. I am open to Your healing and Your empowering arms wrapped securely around me. You will lead me and guide me during this time into a deep loving relationship. Amen.

# 5

# The Best Time to Pray or Meditate

Very early in the morning, while it was still
dark, Jesus got up, left the house and went off
to a solitary place, where he prayed.

—Mark 1:35

In the morning, Lord, you hear my voice; in the
morning I lay my requests before you and wait
expectantly.

—Psalm 5:3

If this is the most challenging step for you, you are not alone!
Most people struggle a bit with finding a regular time to
do the things they want to, including exercise, cooking healthy
meals, and taking time for themselves. It never gets to be a
regular habit because when the time keeps changing, there is a
choice decision being made every day that opens up the option
to say no, not today. There is always an excuse or something
that takes up all the time. If you can commit to this step of
finding a consistent time, you will have the highest possibility
for success. Unlike my diets, which I go on and off of, I rarely
skip my time with God. It is like breathing air to me, essential
for my day.

For the longest time, I struggled to find a regular time to

read the Bible and meditate on the Word of God. It seemed like the morning was not working with getting the four kids ready for school and getting myself ready for work. There just wasn't the time and energy on a daily basis. At night, I was so exhausted that I just wanted to watch TV and fall asleep. So, if you are in that phase of your life right now, I understand! And God understands! Give yourself grace and know that there are times in our lives when this will be more challenging.

However, had I known what I know now, I would have asked God to help me find time for Him. For a long time, my prayer time was very sporadic because I hadn't picked a specific time that worked. I believe there is time in the day, and God will help you carve it out if you are committed to this. First, keep reminding yourself that everyone in your life will benefit from you being more connected to your Creator because you will have more love, joy, peace, patience, kindness, goodness, faithfulness, gentleness, and self-control (Galatians 5:22).

This is not meant to make you feel guilty; it is just to bring the truth forward and increase awareness. The average American spends more than three and a half hours per day watching TV, and most other developed countries are not far behind. So, why is it that we can find this much time to watch TV, but we struggle to find time for God?

I can admit that I have binge-watched many a series, and it was very enjoyable. It is a very passive activity that requires very little effort, which is what we need at times. We just need to be aware that maybe having the time to spend with God may not be the issue. Could it be that because there is some effort involved, we hover on the edge of having and not having the energy to pursue prayer and meditation? Is something else holding you back? Whatever the reason, now is the time to set a goal for yourself to find a small chunk of time; you can always build onto this time as you get more comfortable with it.

So, let's start exploring morning as an option for your prayer and meditation time. Is the morning the best time for you? This is probably the most popular time for prayer and meditation. There is something very grounding about giving that first part of your day to Jesus and starting the day with Him.

It has become my favorite part of the day because it is positive and relational, and I give all my anxiety about the day to Him. Energy levels are not zapped by the workday, and distractions may be fewer.

I understand that not everyone is a morning person. For non-morning people, the Bible verse about Jesus going off early in the morning is not about Jesus reading the Bible and meditating on scripture because he did not have a Bible. He prayed in the morning, at mealtime, and at all times. I believe that starting your day with a prayer in the morning is essential, but it can be a short "Please be with me today in all that I do and say, Lord" prayer.

With that being said, here are some options for times to pray and meditate on scripture and well as some thoughts about pros and cons of each time:

Morning

You have to get up earlier than your normal time. You can do this! The advantages of starting your day with Jesus include asking Him to guide your day from the start. There are more biblical verses about this time for prayer and meditation. Your mind is fresh, and it's a new day.

Midmorning

This is a great time to take a break from work, baby's naptime, or time for a snack. The stress of the morning is off, and you might be more relaxed than early in the morning. Time may be limited to work schedule versus having time to be patient and letting God speak to you. Upcoming events may creep in on your thoughts.

Lunchtime

Eat lunch while reading devotion—and then pray and meditate on the Word. This schedule can really be effective because lunchtime is a pretty regular event, and you can pair it with that. It obviously would not work for those who use a breakroom or have a family to feed. One idea may be to do a devotion with a lunch group and then take fifteen minutes at your desk to pray or meditate if you have a separate space.

Midafternoon: Coffee Break Time

This has a very cozy feeling to me. I've never tried this time, but it sounds great as long as you have this option every day. Most of your workday is over, and you may have work situations to bring to God for help and wisdom.

Evening

This is probably the most relaxed time, but it also can have the most distractions. You also may be tired. If you pick this option, you need to really be devoted to this time. I use evening prayer to thank God for the day and pray for people or situations, but I'm often too tired to sit with my eyes closed without falling asleep.

Middle of the Night

If you wake up in the middle of the night worried about something, give it to God. He wants you to bring it to Him. Sometimes this is the only quiet time in our lives, and God has to use this time to get ahold of you! This is not a good option for anyone, for goodness's sake. I have fallen into that trap before. and it's not a good one.

Whatever option you choose, make a commitment to do it for forty days. Make it your top priority. Know that you will be challenged on this because there are negative forces in the world that will try to interfere. You need to have your guard up. Put on your full armor!

> Finally, be strong in the Lord and in his mighty power. Put on the full armor of God, so that you can take your stand against the devil's schemes. For our struggle is not against flesh and blood, but against the rulers, against the authorities, against the powers of this dark world and against the spiritual forces of evil in the heavenly realms. Therefore put on the full armor of God, so that when the day of evil comes, you may be able to stand your ground, and after you have done everything, to stand. Stand firm then, with the belt of truth buckled around your waist, with the breastplate of righteousness in place, and with your feet fitted with the readiness that comes from the Gospel of peace. In addition to all this, take up the shield of faith, with which you can extinguish all the flaming arrows of the evil one. Take the helmet of salvation and the sword of the Spirit, which is the word of God. And pray in the Spirit on all occasions with all kinds of prayers and requests. With this in mind, be alert and always keep on praying for all the Lord's people. (Ephesians 6:10–18)

Let's explore this armor of God. These are going to be your defense tools when you feel like you don't have the time or energy to pray and meditate. There really are unseen forces trying to vie for your time and attention. How are you going to fight back?

You buckle the belt of truth around your waist by knowing what the truth is. The truth is found in the Word, the Bible, scripture. Picture in your mind wrapping this around your waist and keeping it in your heart.

Your breastplate of righteousness is in place. You are not self-righteous, but you are righteous in that you know God's Word is true and right. When there is a problem, you know that you can go to God and His Word, and the answer will be there.

Your feet are ready for action with the Gospel of peace. I picture putting on shoes that have the power of the Father, Son, and Holy Spirit. I want to put on these shoes every day and run with others who also have these shoes on!

While writing this book, there were countless times where I felt it was a battle of wills. I would want to start writing, but something would come up and try to distract me. I asked my friends to pray for me and the writing of this book. I asked God to help me stay focused and for it to be His words that came from my hands. These prayers were answered because you are reading this book!

I subscribe to several newsletters and devotions online, and one of them spoke about being diligent with the work that God has called you to do. Do at least a little bit every day. I really took this to heart, and every day, I put the pen to the paper or my hands on the computer. I have found that the words just flow when you let God do the talking. He runs the race with us.

When the problems of the world come at you like flaming arrows, the shield of faith extinguishes *all* of them. Expect problems—but be confident that He has given you tools to get through. As the saying adapted from Isaiah 58:11 goes: "If He brings you to it, He will bring you through it."

Lastly, you have a helmet and a sword. This equipment is your preparedness for moving forward toward any goal you set. Be strong and confident. With God's Word, you are prepared.

With your armor on and God by your side, I know that you will succeed!

1. What time of day appears to be the most opportune for success and why?

_____

_____

_____

2. What is a second option and why?

_____

_____

_____

3. Why is it necessary to put on your full armor during this process?

_____

_____

_____

Prayer: Heavenly Father, You are the all-powerful, ever-living God. I see myself having success because You are with me, helping me learn to pray and meditate. Please bless this time together and guard my heart, mind, and spirit. Help me keep my promise to You to spend this time together as a new life skill. In Jesus's name. Amen.

# 6

# How Do I Start?

Now that you have your place picked out, your things ready, and your time decided on, you are ready to start! So, how do we start? If you chose the morning, set your alarm for fifteen minutes—or however long you can spend—earlier than your normal waking time.

Shower and get your coffee and even your breakfast if it won't distract you while you are reading your devotion. Go to your quiet space, and if possible, shut the door.

A good start is just taking a deep breath and asking God to be there with you. You could say something like this: "Father God, I am committing this time to You, for You are my Creator, Redeemer, and Savior. Thank You for this time together and help me open my heart and mind to the message You want to speak to me today."

I like to read my devotion first while I eat a small simple breakfast. Then I look up the Bible verse from the devotion and read the chapter surrounding it. There is often a story around the verse that brings me to a bigger understanding of the scripture, and it adds more depth to the devotion. Then I restate the verse as many times as needed for it to sink in.

Some days, I am very focused, but when I have a lot on my mind, it may take several repetitions. Then I sit quietly and wait for His voice, His comfort, His healing, and His presence.

There are many ways that God speaks to us. Many times, it's someone I need to be praying for. Sometimes it's a warm, calming feeling that comes over me. Other times, it's a positive affirmation about who I am. Occasionally, it's an action plan: "Hey Tami, why don't you write a book about prayer and meditation?" Often, it's about an interaction with people that keeps recurring. Because I have my prayer journal notebook available, I can write down what I am hearing. When I have an opportunity to meet with other people I trust, I can discuss the ideas with them—and they can help me decide whether these are biblically based messages that will bear fruit or not. It is very good to have a journal because you can look back and see how God has answered the prayers.

Included in this book are forty days of devotions. You can start the devotions at any time while reading this book, or wait until you are done, if you want to feel more prepared. This will help you develop a routine for taking time to spend with the Creator. For me, the Father, Son, and Holy Spirit come alive during this time. I read the scripture as many times as need to feel it become part of me. The most common feeling for me is when I feel my shoulders come down a notch as if the stress of the world is being lifted.

The steps that I use are a suggestion based on what works for me. Experiment with different methods until you find the right fit for you. Once you establish a positive routine, you will find that it is easier to focus. Also, the depth of your experience will increase.

I have experimented with another prayer sequence that has a more structured approach. It is similar to the ACTS (adoration, confession, thanksgiving, supplication) sequence, which I also really like, but it includes meditation time. ACBM starts with *adoration* and thanksgiving, *confession* and seeking help, reading a *Bible* verse, and *meditating*. Each of these steps in your prayer time can be long or short as you feel called.

Adoration or praising God could sound something like this: Heavenly Father, I sit before You today acknowledging Your greatness as my Creator, Redeemer, and Savior." This is the most important step because the first commandment is to have no other gods. Putting this first is saying that this is the most important thing in your life.

Thanksgiving is your chance to thank God for all things in your life, including gifts of time, talents, and personal things, all of which are His on loan to us. Thanking Him for your problems is also a way to release them to His power. Gratitude is a very positive experience because it helps you focus on all the aspects of your life.

Some people use a gratitude journal every day to help them stay positive, and some people do a weekly entry. You will have space in your devotional to reflect and practice journaling in this way.

Confession is your time to examine the previous day, week, or past and tell God your concerns about your actions, thoughts, and decisions you've made or are about to make. Ask for forgiveness in anything you see as not what Jesus would have done.

Seeking help means asking Him to intervene in any situation you need help with. Envisioning how God might intervene for you can restore hope for the future. Although your prayers may not be answered exactly how you think, they will be answered in His time, in His way. Often, they are answered beyond our wildest dreams or in ways that make us laugh and shake our heads.

For example, owning a lake cabin was a dream of ours since my husband and I met in college. After twenty-five years of looking at properties, we had resigned it to the fact that we couldn't afford anything we would want to use. We decided to just be thankful for what we had.

The summer we decided we would just visit friends' cabins and stop worrying about finding our place, we stumbled across a tiny cabin with beautiful property. It needed a lot of work, but it was fairly humorous that just as we decided to resign ourselves to "visitor status," God gave us an opportunity. We really felt that it was a gift from God showing us not to worry, a reward for hard work, and that when you take care of the small things He gives you, you will be given more. The cabin is a place where we can have peace and connect even further with our Creator. We share it with family and friends so they can experience another beautiful place that God made, and we get to worship together with whoever is here on Sunday. It is God's cabin that He gave us to enjoy and share.

Bible Verse Memorization

Sometimes I come across a Bible verse that I want to memorize. If you would like to do this, I recommend writing it down on a piece of paper and taking it with you to repeat throughout the day. Repeating it three times throughout the day and then once per day for the next two weeks will embed it in your memory.

Why memorize Bible verses? Having Bible verses in your memory can help you be prepared when struggles in life come up for you or someone you know.

Bible verses in your home can also be a source of positivity. When my husband was diagnosed with cancer, we had Isaiah 58:11 on a plaque. He said that focusing on it really helped him be strong when he was going through treatment.

Meditate

Open your mind to what the Father, Son, and Holy Spirit have to say to you during this time. If your mind wanders to thoughts other than the above steps, gently bring it back to stillness and listen for God's message for you today.

Writing down things that come to mind can help you process messages and gain clarity for calls to action. You may get a message that is meant for you or another person. Calls for action can be tiny things that solve big problems.

Although we are setting a goal to do this, it is not the

amount of time you spend with the Lord; it is making the choice to spend time with Him and listening for His message to you. By setting a goal, we are learning a new habit, and this habit will become a positive part of your daily life.

Setting Goals

Write your goal to start your prayer and meditation time on this date:

_____

_____

- I have set aside this amount of time:

_____

_____

- For forty days! I am so excited for you!
- How are you feeling about setting a goal?

_____

_____

- What routine for prayer and meditation do I want to try first and why?

_____

_____

- What would be a second option and why?

_____

_____

Prayer: Father God, You are above, below, and beside me. Help me develop a good routine designed especially for You and me to connect. As we spend time together, I want to tell You how important You are to me and why I want to spend time with You every day. I know that you can help calm my mind and give me peace. I want to hear Your voice, feel your presence, and see doors opening. Thank You, Father, for this time with You. Help me keep this time sacred. Amen.

# 7
# Why We Use the Bible

**T**he Bible is an ancient book that is considered to be the Holy Scripture of the Christian religion. There are questions about when exactly it was written, but the general consensus is that the Old Testament books were written long before Jesus's time, and the New Testament was written after Jesus died to tell His story and talk about the future. The Bible is one of the most widely read books on earth, and because it has been copied so many times and still contains the same basic information, it is considered to be highly accurate historically. If you haven't read it, this is your invitation. Besides having an answer to virtually all life's questions, it has more drama and human-interest stories than most novels.

If you need a place to start, consider reading one of the first Gospels of Matthew, Mark, Luke, or John. Some people just start from Genesis and go all the way through. There are 929 chapters in the Old Testament and 260 chapters in the New Testament—so you can do it in a year if you read three or four chapters per day.

Regularly reading the Bible, which is God's Word, feeds our minds, redirects our thinking from the world to Him, and helps us grow in maturity. Here are ten reasons to read the Bible every day:

1. The Bible has authority; it is God's Word to us. Before we had the Bible, people were dependent on hearing from God through listening to other people. God gave us the Bible so that we can refer to it when we need to hear His Word.

2. The Bible teaches us to love. There are more than one hundred Bible verses about love. My favorite is 1 Corinthians 13:4–5, which talks about love being patient and kind. I have considered this as a tattoo because I need to be reminded of this!

3. The Bible teaches us rules. Rules are a necessary thing for order and peace. Sometimes, we don't like rules, but they help us keep our homes, cities, and country safe.

4. The Bible leads us on the right path. When we have to make decisions, scripture can help us to make choices that will help and not harm. There are so many choices for us to make every single day, and we need a reference tool when questions about decisions come up. Better yet, embedding scripture in your mind by memorizing verses will allow you to keep them with you all the time.

5. The Bible helps us learn to serve others and put the needs of others first. In our society, which focuses on I, me, and more I, it is good to have messages about helping others.

6. The Bible reminds us to forgive. There are many forgiveness stories in the Bible, but a few favorites are Acts 7, Matthew 18, Genesis 45, John 8, and 1 Samuel 24. I have yet to forgive someone seventy-seven times, but I am working on it!

7. The Bible teaches us to pray and meditate. We know all about that now, don't we?

8. The Bible helps us not worry. Jesus again and again tells us not to be anxious or worry. This reassurance throughout the Bible is there for a reason; we worry too much about our health, finances, family, and daily life.

9. The Bible provides hope. When all is not going well, we need a message to help us find hope, and the Bible is full of reassurance that God is with us and will never leave us.
10. The Bible leads us to our heavenly home. When the end of life comes, and it will come for all of us, we can be reassured that we are going to a place that is good because we have developed a relationship with our Creator—and He is preparing a place for us (John 14:2–3).

You can forget any negative things that you may have said to yourself with these bible verses:

- I am not good enough. Psalm 139:14

  _____

  _____

- I can't be forgiven. Ephesians 4:32

  _____

  _____

- I don't make good decisions. Proverbs 12:15

  _____

  _____

- I am not lovable. 1 Peter 5:66-7

  _____

  _____

- I am unsavable. 2 Cor 5:21

  _____

  _____

- I am hopeless. Psalm 40:1-3

 

The Bible has stories of people who had all of these problems and more! You are worthy of all the love, hope, joy, and peace the Father provides. Our enemy would like nothing more than to get in our heads and stop us from living empowered lives. When we take the time to read the Bible, pray, and meditate on the Word, the kingdom of God opens wide for us.

- What negative statements do you need to take captive and change to a more positive thought?

 

- If you are new to Bible reading, where would you like to start reading the Bible?

 

- Do you have a favorite book of the Bible or Bible story and why?

 

Prayer: Heavenly Father, thank You for giving us the Bible. Help us use this tool to shift our negative thoughts to positive solutions in our lives. We are learning about how You love us, Your goodness, and how you provide for us by reading Your Word. There is nothing to fear because You have us in Your care. Amen.

# 8

# Common Roadblocks

Now that we have the "how" and "why" of meditation and prayer time, let's talk about the "why nots," or the roadblocks that prevent us from having what we want. Having knowledge about how to deal with setbacks gives you tools to put in your toolbox that can help you stay focused on your goal.

What if you have all your ducks in a row, set your alarm twenty minutes early, and then you find out your dog made a huge mess that you have to clean up? We need to be prepared for things to happen. The best thing you can do is thank God for everything in your life—even the problems.

We are not going to win this battle if we become upset or frustrated about our prayer time not going perfectly. We have to have an "oh-well" attitude for times like this and know that God is there in every moment with you, comforting you.

When you look at how Jesus did His meditation and prayer time, He sometimes waited until an event was over. For example, after He fed the five thousand (Matthew 14:13–21), He went away to pray. I picture Him taking that time to thank God for the problem and for the miracle of being able to feed all those people.

Sometimes categorizing possible problems can help you compartmentalize them and more easily access solutions. Here are some examples and suggestions in the event that you need a tool to help you stay on track:

Time Stealers

When something is thrown at you during your time set aside for God, thank Him for it and take care of it like you are working for the Lord. Depending on your situation, try to use what time you have left to meditate on the verse in your devotional.

Keep your same time and ask God to help you. You can take your scripture verse with you and repeat it throughout the day—or try to find another time if it continues to happen repeatedly. Have confidence that God will help you find the best time to meet with Him.

Distractions

We all have thoughts that distract us during this time. When you notice your mind wandering, be kind to yourself and gently bring your mind back to what you were reading, praying, or meditating on. This is normal.

Check your thoughts and know that these might be calls to action or prayers for people. If it is a call to action, write it down and prayerfully consider it. If it is a God-driven thought, you will likely repeatedly be called or get a confirmation in some way. A good way to check this is to describe it to another trusted Christian to see if they believe it is in line with biblical truth. Any prayers can also be written down in your journal, and it is very comforting to look back and see how God answers all prayers.

Know that distractions will occur during your prayer and meditation time. Be prepared to deal with them by bringing your mind back to scripture, writing it down, or thinking thoughtfully about if it is something that God wants you to take action on.

## Not Hearing Anything

Many people have really high expectations of what this experience is going to look like and feel like, possibly due to what is seen in the media or on TV. I don't doubt that it could happen because I believe that an angel did appear to Mary to announce that she was going to be a mama. I have never seen visions of angels, light shows, and supernatural occurrences during this time.

Initially, I remember being somewhat anxious, and I did not feel a lot. The messages and feelings were very subtle. Over time, my senses have become more tuned in, and I have had so many experiences that there is no doubt in my mind that God is there with me, hearing my prayers and helping me through life.

His answers to prayers are also more obvious looking back than in the moment, and they are often humorous and beyond expectations. For example, when my husband, Eric, and I were praying and exploring doing mission work globally, we looked at many different places, but I really did not want to go to Africa. That was not a place I felt safe to go to, based on what I had seen on television.

Then our daughter Shana was sent there for Peace Corps work. I was terrified about what was going to happen to her, but I kept hearing stories of all the need there and the experiences she was having. She helped us plan a mission trip there, and it was one of the most amazing experiences of our lives.

Spending time with the wonderful people there really opened my eyes to their beautiful culture and faith. It is actually very humorous to me how scared I was then—and what a great experience we had. My favorite memory was reading the Christmas story about Jesus's birth to a group of orphaned children. We actually went back a second time and are open to going again as our relationships develop and needs become known to us.

Through prayer, God gave us courage when there was

fear, truth when there was ignorance, and direction when we asked for a calling. So, remember, when you are feeling like you aren't hearing anything, God may be working in ways you don't realize immediately.

Plateaus

There are times when you will feel the communication is clear, and at other times, there might be a plateau. This is when your mind is quietly absorbing God's Word. Many times, right as you are ready to give up, a door opens.

Psalm 119:33 says, "Just tell me what to do, and I will do it, Lord." But don't play the game of God telling you and then you deciding whether to do it or not. God doesn't play games, but He is patient—and He will give you interesting challenges. Until you engage in what God has told you to do already, he is not likely to teach you more things.

You can include in your prayer to give you strength to follow His directions joyfully, continually, and completely for the rest of your life. We will not be perfect all the time, but you will be blessed when you take one step at a time and do what you are being asked to do.

Overconfidence

Some people feel like they don't need God to solve their problems. They have good jobs, their kids are doing well on their own, and they don't need a higher power. If the devil can convince a person that they don't need God in their lives, that is called deception. You are deceived to believe that doing life alone is just as good as doing life with Jesus. This overconfidence and self-righteousness can rob people of the desire to grow in their faith. My husband always says, "What do you have to lose? If I believe and there is a heaven, I'm going there. But if I don't believe, I won't go either way." Good point.

I also have experienced life without putting God first, and I know that I can do so much more when I submit my problems and life to Him. When you enlist the Father, Son, and Holy Spirit, there is nothing you can't do. You can either try to do everything on your own or surrender that thought like Jesus did on the cross when He said, "Father, into thy hands I commit my spirit" (Luke 23:46). There is something powerful when you get to that point where you need to surrender something to God and enlist His help.

I choose to believe because in my experience, there is no other relationship that is as accepting, forgiving, peaceful, hopeful, and joyful as my relationship with my Creator. The relationship is amazing, and it's different but equally amazing for every single person. When I look at the world and all that is in it, there is no doubt in my mind that that a Creator exists. I want to be part of His plan. When my last day on earth comes, He will welcome me into His open arms.

Lack of Confidence

Others feel that they are a hopeless case and that God is so sick and tired of hearing all the problems. Ask God to fill the gaps in your life. We all have weaknesses, and the reason for this is so that we can lean on Him. These problems are not random mistakes; they are handpicked blessings that are designed for your growth.

Have you ever met someone who seems to have had a host of problems, but they are the most interesting people to talk to because of all their experiences? They seem to have an extra dose of empathy, and you can be totally real with them because there are no pretenses. Their experiences have made them the most loving and warm people who you want in your life.

The bottom line is that a lack of confidence can grow into humbleness, which is a virtue. Mother Teresa lived her life with people in poverty, and she was the epitome of humility. She is now revered among the saints. God wants to have a relationship with you, and He will help you solve problems in His way and in His time. Pray for God to help you view problems as opportunities to rely more fully on Him.

Anxiety

This is a very common roadblock for many people. You just sit down to spend time with God, and the responsibilities of the day start popping up in your mind. Focusing on our Creator is very difficult when you are mentally trying to keep track of the things you need to do. There is clinical anxiety, which I do not claim to have the answers for, but I am talking about feeling anxiety. This is why God gave us scratch paper.

When something comes to mind about the upcoming day, write it down. You can also have a to-do list on your phone, but that can lead to checking other things on your phone—so the preference for this situation is old-fashioned paper and pen. When it's written down, you can stop thinking about it until after you are done with your devotions.

This also works when you are having anxiety about the next day or have trouble getting to sleep at night. Keep a notebook and pen on your nightstand. Write down your to-dos for the next day and then say, "Jesus, peace."

Although self-sufficiency is looked at as highly desired in our culture, we know that if we humble ourselves, He will lift us up. Reliance on Him produces abundant life.

To sum up this chapter about roadblocks, thank God for your time stealers, distractions, overconfidence or lack of confidence, silence, plateaus, and anxiety. These roadblocks are all creating a wiser, more patient, kinder, and more caring you.

What are three possible roadblocks that you anticipate—and how are you going to deal with them so that they do not prevent you from spending great quality time with your Creator?

1. _____

_____

_____

2. _____

_____

_____

3. _____

_____

_____

Prayer: Heavenly Father, I give these roadblocks to You, casting them into Your care. I know I will have trouble in this life, but with You as my Guide and Counselor, I know that I will be able to handle them, learn from them, and continue on my faith journey. Help me use my experiences to encourage others. Amen.

# 9

# Not All Meditation Is the Same

Each human will approach meditation in their own way, based on their individual experiences and what is going on in their life at the time. That is what is so beautiful about it; it is unique and a rich experience that is initiated by you and shaped by God.

However, not all meditation focuses on our Creator. For example, yoga meditation, while it is very good, does not necessarily share all the benefits that spiritual meditation does because the focus tends to be on the self. When you spend time with Jesus, your mind is open to going beyond yourself, which is how Jesus lived and calls us to live. Jesus was always looking for ways to help others.

Meditation on the Word is a way to honor your Creator. He is ultimately in charge of all time and all things. Of course, there are a plethora of benefits for you that come along with this, including peace of mind, centeredness, relationship, love, focus, healing, awareness, and the list goes on. Your benefits are a result of putting Him first—blessings from your heavenly Father.

When meditating, your awareness starts with God, and then it naturally flows to others. An example of "going beyond yourself" as Jesus lived was when my husband and I learned about how to handle our money. When were younger, we struggled financially, always living paycheck to paycheck. We did not understand the concept of tithing, which is setting aside a percentage of your income to go beyond yourself. It was putting trust in God, that in making a sacrifice to Him, we would have our needs met.

When you go beyond yourself, you are giving Him control. A whole new world opened up to us financially, mentally, and spiritually. You allow Him to use you and your resources of time, money, and talent for His purposes.

While some meditation focuses on self-improvement, Christian meditation focuses on our Creator, our relationship with Him, and what he calls us to do. He is the one true God who deserves our focused attention and praise. Sacrificing time is a form of worship, and the benefit is the relationship. When you spend time with someone, you develop a relationship with them.

Have you noticed how your family members or friends start taking on characteristics of the people they hang out with? You can start taking on the characteristics of Jesus by hanging out with Him, praising Him, and meditating on His Word. You can show Him that He holds the number one spot in your heart and mind. The true way to self-improvement is to become more like Jesus. The way to become more like Jesus is to spend time with Him through prayer and meditation.

All meditation is not the same. When you incorporate Jesus into your meditation, it goes in a totally new spiritual direction, fulfilling a part of you that is longing for growth and healing. Will you be standing, sitting, or lying down? Will you pray first or read scripture first? Whether you go to a mountain or in a closet, God is waiting for you to develop your meditation routine with Him.

1. How do you think this type of meditation will be different than other forms of meditation?

_____

_____

2. In what ways have you experienced—or would you like to experience—going beyond yourself?

_____

_____

3. Have you ever noticed someone taking on the characteristics of someone in a positive or negative way?

_____

_____

4. How will your meditation be different than anyone else's meditation?

_____

_____

Prayer: Heavenly Father, You are my Creator and Redeemer. I know that this prayer and meditation time with You is a healthy thing for me emotionally, physically, and spiritually because by spending time with You and asking for Your help, I will become more like You. Please bless this time and hear and answer my prayers. Amen.

# 10

# The Difference Prayer and Meditation Can Make in Your Life

The art of spending time with God invites you to open up your mind to a new relationship with your Creator. Giving your time, bowing down before Him, and surrendering your mind, body, and soul allows you a new freedom from the strife of trying to control everything yourself.

Trusting Him with your life and your plans by allowing Him to fill in the gaps of your skills gives you relief from anxiety and stress of having to have it all and do it all.

A good example of this is my writing this book. I am not a journalist, so I am battling the fear that what I am writing, or the way I am writing it, is not good enough. I have to trust that my gaps of skills can and will be filled by the power of the Holy Spirit and that this book is truly inspired by God. He will also provide people who will help me when my skills fall short. When doubt seeps in like a leaky basement wall, I give it to Him—and then I don't have to worry about it.

Allowing Him to open doors and pave the way gives a sense of peace that you don't have to create everything and make things happen by yourself. My favorite Bible verse is Matthew 7:7. "Ask and you shall receive, seek and you shall find, knock and the door will be opened unto you." He wants you to ask, and He wants to open doors for you. Sometimes it doesn't feel that way, but He will only open doors for you that are good for you—and the ones you want to open may not be the right ones.

Praying and meditating on the Word is healthy for you mentally, physically, and financially. Praying for Him to give you the courage to tithe and being careful about what you watch on television, who you hang out with, and what you eat allows Him the space to nudge you in the right direction when choices are being made.

When we give ourselves to Him, it shines light into our hearts and allows us to share His light with others. When you see positive things happening in your life, you can share your good news with others so that they can benefit as well. It is so satisfying to see others' lives moving in a positive direction.

We have so many examples of this when the Adult and Teen Challenge group comes to our church. We hear personal stories of how becoming a Christian and relinquishing their addictions to Jesus completely turned their lives around. They are stories of surrender, trust, opening, sharing, giving, allowing, and focusing. These are all key components of spending time with God. He is in control. He fills the gaps. He creates opportunities. He loves and gives and smiles down on you when you allow Him into your heart and life.

Socrates said. "Life contains but two tragedies, one is not to get your heart's desire; the other is to get it." When I was young, I prayed for getting things that I desired a lot. Sometimes I got them, sometimes not, and I could never figure out if God was listening or if it was just fate.

As life went on, my focus shifted more to people, situations, and events in life. I found such joy and relief by giving my cares to Jesus during my prayer time. He is my best friend, and He is always there for me, giving me positive affirmations, wrapping me in loving arms, and listening to every fear, anxiety, hope, and dream.

Reading God's Word renews my mind. He knows exactly what I need so that I can look at each day's events as gifts from which to learn and grow. He will give you the words and actions you need for the day as He prepares each and every moment. I can feel my shoulders relax as the anxiety leaves my mind and body.

When you bring the sacrifice of your time to Jesus, you create a sacred space around you. This space is enveloped in the love, joy, and peace that only He can bring to you and your life. This time is such a wise investment because it is the only way you will be fully equipped to face the challenges of the day.

Do not be in a hurry to dive into your day. Give the Lord His time and push back on the pressures of the day, knowing that you are putting a deposit into your heavenly savings account. The Lord will bless you, strengthen you, and give you peace and wisdom that you will bring with you today and tomorrow.

When I was nineteen, I found a lump in my breast. When I was thirty-five, I had cervical cancer. Then in my fifties, I had several skin cancer episodes that required surgery. If you have ever had a doctor say the word "cancer" to you, you know it is a very scary word—and you will never take life for granted again.

Why I am continually being reminded of this, I do not know, but one thing for sure is that I don't want to waste a day. I lived way too much of my life being introverted and scared of everything that when I heard the word "cancer," it really made me live my life differently.

I admit I have taken that to an extreme at times. I have skydived, scuba-dived, ran a full marathon, swam in a shark cage, ate a mopani worm (look that up!) and walked with a live adult lion. I do not have the desire to do things like skydiving again, even though it was probably the most exhilarating thing I've ever done, but I do want to live life to the fullest.

Doing some of these things was symbolic of the new me and helps me to believe I don't have to be the timid, shy person I once was. I can be brave, and I can respond "yes" when God asks me to do something even if it's out of my comfort zone. When I see him face-to-face, I will thank him for bringing me from timid and shy to bold and courageous when I needed to be.

What I did think was interesting at the time was that I could jump out of an airplane, but at the time, I wasn't bold enough to talk about Jesus. Well, obviously that has changed! Each of these things in our lives is preparing us for the next step in God's plan. I had to go through this phase in order to get to the person God wanted me to be.

Reading the Bible every day and meditating is important to do every day. It gives you clarity about what you are doing with your life, but there can be times when the Bible can have seemingly conflicting messages:

> In the same way let your light shine before others, that they may see your good deeds and glorify your Father in heaven. (Matthew 5:16)

This verse can be perplexing because there are other verses such as Matthew 6:1–2, which says, "Be careful not to practice your righteousness in front of others to be seen by then. If you do, you will have no reward from your Father in Heaven." It then goes on to say give to the poor in secret, then your Father will reward you. The Bible is full of "this … ands." It says one thing and then has another verse that sounds like a contradiction, when in fact, it is both. For example, with these two verses, both can coexist. It is important to demonstrate to others how to do good deeds and show how Christians are the hands and feet of Jesus, but there is a right and wrong way to do this. It's all about the intent. Are you doing what you are doing to make yourself look good or to be seen? The reason for doing good deeds should be to glorify God and not for appearances or for rules. If it is a God-driven, Holy Spirit-empowered, and "Jesus with skin on" deed, then it is done for the right reasons.

To test this, when you feel the pull to do something, pray about it and think about your motivations. Ask God to help you and share your ideas with other Christians who can help you. At one of the first Great River Family Promise meetings, one of the women said, "Why are you doing this? You are doing this for the wrong reasons." This really deflated my energy because I started to question my intent.

I took some time to examine my motivations and retraced my steps. I realized it was a God-inspired deed, and I was not doing it to be seen. My only motivation was to help homeless families, which was put on my heart, and then the energy was given to me to continue.

I believe this cause truly was divine, because looking back, how could a mom of four children, working full-time have the time and energy to start a homeless shelter program? The individuals in the group were all inspired by God to do His work. So, the key is to do good deeds to glorify your Father.

Do everything in love, do everything as if you are doing it for God, and give generously to the poor—and you will receive the reward from God. We do not deserve this reward, but we are his children, and He loves to reward us just as we love to give our children the best.

What are three benefits you can anticipate from making prayer and meditation part of your routine?

1. _____

_____

_____

2. _____

_____

_____

3. _____

   _____

   _____

# 11

# Forty Days of Devotions

**H**ere is a devotional to help you get started establishing a routine of spending time with God. It is structured to focus on your relationship with the Father, Son, and Holy Spirit. It uses a scripture verse to help you meditate on the teachings of Jesus. It then poses a question and gives you space to write what you hear God saying to you. Please use this as a guide and not a fence to box you in.

The Bible verse is the main idea so you can just meditate on that or read the devotional and then meditate on the whole message. It is purposely written in a variety of styles—with some history, some emotional stories, and some devotions that are just to the point—in hopes that you will discover what type of prayer, meditation, or devotion you prefer. The goal is to help you open the door of communication, ask questions such as what was going on during biblical times, and determine how we can apply this to our lives today. There is a door to your heart and mind that you have to open. Ask Him, and He will help you open it. Your relationship with Him will be unique and beautiful. God bless you!

## Day 1

> Ask and it will be given to you; seek and you will
> find; knock and the door will be opened to you.
> —Matthew 7:7

Jesus said these words to encourage His disciples and to open communication. Up until the time of the New Testament, God had been perceived as very authoritarian and not approachable for the average person. These words were so important for them—and continue to be now—since we can sometimes feel some distance starting to form in our relationship with Jesus. The Lord is awaiting your time with Him. Meet with the Lord every day in the early morning splendor and in the evening quietness. Because you have felt drawn toward Him, while others turn over for more sleep or turn on the TV, you are seeking a higher calling. "When you seek My face, you will find Me. When you ask, you will receive. When you knock, the door will open." The Lord is waiting to bless you.

What do you need to ask God for today?

_____

_____

_____

_____

_____

_____

# Day 2

> Trust in Him at all times, you people; pour out
> your hearts to Him, for God is our refuge.
> —Psalm 62:8

David was in a predicament. People were lying about him and trying to topple him as king. He had strength in God, who was his rock and salvation. If you are lucky, you have a best friend who you can tell almost anything to without them judging you. Did you catch the word *almost* in that sentence? Human beings are not meant to be perfect or always able to handle anything that comes our way. When we put all of our problems on another person, we are expecting them to be superhuman. No one can be everything for you. That is not true with Jesus, you *can* tell Him *anything* because He knows everything anyway! He is always there for us, and you can trust Him at *all* times. Pour out your heart to Him and let Him be your shelter.

What is God saying to you in this moment?

_____

_____

_____

_____

_____

_____

_____

# Day 3

> Finally, brothers and sisters, whatever is true, whatever is noble, whatever is right, whatever is pure, whatever is lovely, whatever is admirable— if anything is excellent or praiseworthy—think about such things.
>
> —Philippians 4:8

The Philippians were described as kind, generous people, and Paul seemed to enjoy being with them. He called them brothers and sisters, but they were not without their struggles. They were tempted by their stomachs and all earthly things, just as we are today. God wants our hearts and minds to be filled with good things. The world seems to have another agenda. We can make good choices about what we listen to and watch throughout our days. We can also be careful about who we spend time with, which will influence how we speak and act. God delights in us finding excellent and praiseworthy things to do and hanging out with lovely and loving people.

What is something that can make God's light shine brighter in you?

_____

_____

_____

_____

_____

_____

# Day 4

> Let the message of Christ dwell among you richly
> as you teach and admonish one another with all
> wisdom through psalms, hymns and songs form
> the Spirit, singing to God with gratitude in your
> hearts.
>
> —Colossians 3:16

There is direction in your life that only a higher power can provide. Letting Christ dwell in your heart gives life, wisdom, and peace. What joy to share this positivity with others through group worship. Scripture offers a road map for living that leads to salvation. Life can sometimes be hard, but we can continue to put one foot in front of the other. May we be open to suggestions from others when we need it.

Who is God bringing to your attention?

_____

_____

_____

_____

_____

_____

_____

_____

# Day 5

> Jesus replied "Love the Lord your God with all your heart and with all your soul and with all your mind."
>
> —Matthew 22:37

I say this verse daily because God is the most important thing in my life, but I know I fall short of it because of my humanness. It takes huge, conscious effort to love with all your heart, soul, and mind. I can pray for help and forgiveness because I know that He is worthy of all praise, and I am trying to give it to Him.

The Lord smiles down on us when we submit our weakness to Him, and He will fill any gaps we have. We do not need to worry about our imperfections—just submit to God our needs and then bask in His love. This mutual love relationship is healing and empowering.

How can you show love to God?

_____

_____

_____

_____

_____

_____

_____

## Day 6

> Therefore, holy brothers and sisters, who share
> in the heavenly calling, fix your thoughts on
> Jesus, whom we acknowledge as our apostle and
> high priest.
>
> —Hebrew 3:1

Sometimes it's hard to picture yourself as a holy brother or sister
with a heavenly calling, but you have a special role on this earth.
Your presence in any given situation changes the trajectory of a
conversation or action. You have a message to bring to others.
Fixing your thoughts on Jesus will help you do the right thing
in your activities today and give you the words to help others.

What prayer is God putting on your heart?

_____

_____

_____

_____

_____

_____

_____

_____

## Day 7

> And now, dear children, continue in Him, so that when He appears, we may be confident and unashamed before Him at his coming.
>
> —1 John 2:28

Jesus is going to appear; does that make you feel happy in anticipation or some other feeling? Jesus is going to come, and He loves you the way you are because He was there when everything was being created—and you are one of His dear children. Of course, we have things that we are not proud of; we were created to have the ability to make choices, and we all make mistakes. We will not be perfect; Jesus is the only perfect one. It is right to feel remorse about wrongdoing, but forgiveness is there to be used and not to sit unused. We can be confident and unashamed at His coming. We are forgiven and "continue in Him."

What does the phrase "continue in Him" mean to you?

_____

_____

_____

_____

_____

_____

_____

## Day 8

> We have this hope as an anchor for the soul,
> firm and secure.
>
> —Hebrews 6:19

When life tugs us away from Jesus as our center, He has an anchor on our soul, tugging us back to Him. This is a very large anchor, bigger than any ship that has ever sailed, firm and secure. Waves of life cause every emotion from happiness to fear, to anxiety, to joy. Every night we can rest comfortably knowing we have a choice to put our hands on the rope and pull toward our anchor, Jesus. Pray away any anxiety by saying. "Jesus, come and pull me back to Your safe arms."

What is God saying to you in this moment?

_____

_____

_____

_____

_____

_____

_____

_____

# Day 9

> Satisfy us in the morning with your unfailing love, that we may sing for joy and be glad all our days.
>
> —Psalm 90:14

Unfailing love is so comforting. His love is not like human love, which can be fickle and imperfect. And we will also have days where we are not singing for joy. Knowing we have this blanket of love over us each and every day can give us a boost so that we can put a smile on our faces even in times of trouble. When we hear words like "cancer" or "divorce," our minds immediately go to places of uncertainty. We don't know what the future holds, and this is never a comforting place to be. Our God gives us hope for the future. He knows that we suffer, and He wants to let us know that there will be a day where we can sing for joy again and be glad. But for now, today, His blanket of love will cover us and give us comfort.

How is God telling you He loves you?

_____

_____

_____

_____

_____

_____

# Day 10

> But he said to me, "My grace is sufficient for
> you, for my power is made perfect in weakness."
> —2 Corinthians 12:9

I don't love the fact that we need grace. I am a person who would love to be perfect, but clearly, I am not. We all know people who seem perfect, but they are not. And unfortunately, the reality is that there are probably people who don't like us because they think we are perfect! Thank goodness we have grace. When we submit our imperfect selves to Jesus, He uses His power to do things beyond what we could do. His power will not be used unless we submit our weakness to Him. It's like having electricity but never turning on the lights. How wonderful that we have this friend who is a constant source of help when we need it.

How is God using you to do things you wouldn't be able to do on your own?

_____

_____

_____

_____

_____

_____

_____

# Day 11

> Therefore, do not worry about tomorrow, for tomorrow will worry about itself. Each day has enough trouble of its own.
>
> —Matthew 6:34

You step on something and need stitches in your foot—or your car breaks down, and then you start to worry about what is going to happen next. Every person on earth has things to worry about, and we are all wired differently. Some people seem to thrive on stress, but most people do not—and some seem to simmer in it until they are ill. Tomorrow will worry about itself, the Bible says. What if you shed that worry? Would that change the trajectory of events? We know through medical science that letting go of stress will help you physically, mentally, and emotionally. As the saying goes, let go and let God. As you sit in His presence, let your shoulders fall down, fully relax, and let Him take control.

What worry, anxiety, or stress can God help you with today?

_____

_____

_____

_____

_____

_____

# Day 12

> God did this so that they would seek Him and perhaps reach out for Him, and find Him, though he is not far from any one of us.
>
> —Acts 17:27–28

God is all around us, and He is waiting for us to seek Him. He created the earth and all that is in it perfectly for us. Whether inside or outside, God is there. When you are outside, look around; it is easy to see that everything was made for our eyes and all senses. The sunset and the stars at night are a feast for our eyes. The miracle of birth and the diversity of the animals on our planet—He shows his divine power with the complexity of nature. Appreciating this is a way to reach out and find Him.

How can you seek or reach out to God today?

_____

_____

_____

_____

_____

_____

_____

_____

## Day 13

> Some trust in chariots and some in horses, but
> we trust in the name of the Lord our God.
> —Psalm 20:7

Trust is a funny thing. You can place trust in many things,
such as a spouse, that they won't do anything to tarnish your
relationship. You can trust family members to help you in times
of need or that coworkers they will do their part of a project. You
can trust that your house is going to protect you from storms
or your car will protect you from getting hurt in an accident.
The car starts, the lights turn on, and the fridge light goes off
when you shut the door, right? There is still a chance that these
things will fail, but God does not fail. He is the everlasting,
ever-living God who is, was, and always will be. There is no
worry when we can rest knowing that we can fully trust Him
with our lives. We don't have to trust in our government or any
objects or humans when we are His children.

What is God saying to you in this moment?

_____

_____

_____

_____

_____

_____

# Day 14

> "For I know the plans I have for you," declares
> the Lord, "plans to prosper you and not to harm
> you, plans to give you hope and a future."
> —Jerimiah 29:11

Sometimes we get so stressed about decisions that it affects our attitudes, our sleep, and our relationships. We cannot ruin God's plan for us, but we can let things get to us, like retirement plans, whether it's safe to go out during a pandemic, or whether I am helping or hurting my child by supporting them financially. Having a higher power to trust in these times and knowing that He has a plan for me makes all the difference. I can let go and let God. He will gently nudge me in the right direction. He will make my path straight. He will lead and guide me to the place He wants me to go. And when I stumble, He will catch me and even carry me if needed. My life is not over, and it is not dull or boring. It is full of experiences, big and little, that are all part of a plan—a plan to prosper me.

How can you let go and let God at this time in your life?

_____

_____

_____

_____

_____

_____

# Day 15

> My son, if you accept my words and store up my commands within you, turning your ear to wisdom and applying your heart to understanding—indeed, if you call out for insight and cry aloud for understanding, and if you look for it as for silver and search for it as for hidden treasure.
>
> —Proverbs 2:1–4

Reading scripture and meditating on it is the way to become wise beyond human capability. The Word has truth and light in it, and when we familiarize, memorize, and store it in our hearts, we give the Father, Son, and the Holy Spirit dominion over our thoughts, words, and actions. We no longer are as easily controlled or steered by earthly desires. Scripture is a treasure to be sought by us. We can choose to live independent lives, and God will always love and care for us like a prodigal child. But choosing to seek Him, spending time with Him, and allowing that space for Him to move you is going to give you a new energy and thought process to benefit everyone around you. This is a relationship that is natural because He created us to worship and adore Him.

How does reading God's Word make you feel?

_____

_____

_____

_____

_____

## Day 16

> Those who look to Him are radiant; their faces
> are never covered with shame.
>> —Psalm 34:5

Every day brings a set of challenges, some small and some that seem insurmountable. We succeed, and we fail. When we look to Jesus for help and forgiveness and to give thanksgiving and praise, our faces become "radiant," which means shining or glowing brightly. How can you be thankful and then have a downcast face? You can't! I always want to be around people who are happy more. Thankfulness and forgiveness give you a cheerful countenance that will be contagious to others.

What situation in your life do you need to give to God so that you can have that radiant glow?

_____

_____

_____

_____

_____

_____

_____

# Day 17

Take delight in the Lord, and He will give you
the desires of your heart.

—Psalm 37:4

He wants to give you all your dreams. We should balance this
with the fact that He is our divine Creator, who deserves all the
respect that is due Him. With joy and submission, communicate
with Him by praying and listening.

What desire or dream is God putting on your heart?

_____

_____

_____

_____

_____

_____

_____

_____

_____

## Day 18

> If we confess our sins, He is faithful and just and will forgive us our sins and purify us from all unrighteousness.
>
> —1 John 1:9

A man in the grocery store allowed me to go ahead of him because I only had one item, and there was a long line. I said, "Well, you did your good deed for the day."

He said, "Oh, I'm not going to heaven."

I was taken aback, and I said, "Oh, I don't think so. You're a nice guy." Thinking back, I wish I had said more, but I have to trust that he heard what was needed. We are forgiven and pure.

For what thought, word, or deed do you need forgiveness?

_____

_____

_____

_____

_____

_____

_____

_____

_____

# Day 19

> Worship the Lord with gladness; come before
> Him with joyful songs.
>
> —Psalm 100:2

Even though there is so much struggle and hurt in the world, we can rejoice because we are saved! Let loose your inhibitions and pick a song to sing to the Lord alone. He will love to hear your voice because He created it uniquely.

What victory do you need to celebrate with God?

_____

_____

_____

_____

_____

_____

_____

_____

_____

_____

## Day 20

> I will sacrifice a thank offering to you and call
> on the name of the Lord.
>
> —Psalm 116:17

Giving in the name of the Lord opens a window of blessing onto you. I can honestly say I have never heard of a person who has sacrificed time, talent, or money in the name of the Lord and regretted it. Tithing, doing mission work, or helping a neighbor in need are all ways to make offerings.

What are some sacrifices of time, talent, or money that you could make?

_____

_____

_____

_____

_____

_____

_____

_____

_____

_____

# Day 21

> For it is by grace you have been saved, through faith-and this is not from yourselves, it is the gift of God.
>
> —Ephesians 2:8

By grace and through faith, we are saved. It is a gift. Thank goodness because without that gift, I would not be saved. I am constantly falling short of being like Jesus, our role model for life. Take this gift and remind yourself whenever you are feeling unworthy or "less than." You are God's child; you are saved.

How is God telling you He loves you?

_____

_____

_____

_____

_____

_____

_____

_____

_____

## Day 22

> Be strong and courageous. Do not be afraid
> or terrified because of them, for the Lord your
> God goes with you; He will never leave you nor
> forsake you.
>
> —Deuteronomy 31:6

These are words of Moses to the people of Israel, but they apply to you as well. You are strong and courageous because you have the love of Jesus in your heart. You have nothing to fear because you know the way to salvation is through faith in God. You are never alone because God goes with you every day.

How is God using you to do things you wouldn't be able to do on your own?

_____

_____

_____

_____

_____

_____

_____

_____

# Day 23

> Now may the Lord of peace Himself give you
> peace at all times and in every way.
> —2 Thessalonians 3:16

Paul wrote these words at a time where there were people who were being "idle and disruptive." There were busybodies. He basically told them to get back to work and earn a living. He told them not to hang out with them or regard them as enemies; instead, they should warn them as fellow believers. This is such a good lesson for today when we have challenges with our economy and jobs.

How can we promote peace and harmony among our neighbors?

_____

_____

_____

_____

_____

_____

_____

_____

_____

# Day 24

> Now faith is being sure of what we hope for and
> certain of what we do not see.
> —Hebrews 11:1

So many stories in the Bible refer to people having faith that
God would provide, including Noah, Sarah, Abraham, Moses,
and David, even when they could not see the future. Many of
us have ancestors who, by faith, came to a new land to make a
better life. We do not see heaven, but we have hope and faith
that this is our destiny. Whatever happens in this life, I am
certain that we will be made perfect.

What action does God want you to take today?

_____

_____

_____

_____

_____

_____

_____

_____

# Day 25

> Yet a time is coming and has now come when the true worshippers will worship the Father in the Spirit and in truth, for they are the kind of worshippers the Father seeks. God is spirit, and his worshippers must worship in the Spirit and in truth.
>
> —John 4:23–24

Worshipping is very important in the faith journey. Worshipping "in spirit" might mean that the Holy Spirit stirs or inspires your heart toward God. Worship in truth includes biblical soundness with scripture as the truth. We worship God with sincerity and rooted in scripture as the Father seeks us to be called "true worshippers."

What is God saying to you in this moment?

_____

_____

_____

_____

_____

_____

_____

_____

# Day 26

> Taste and see that the Lord is good; blessed are
> those who take refuge in Him.
>
> —Psalm 34:8

This is an invitation for everyone who is struggling to find refuge and hope. It is important that we invite others into our homes and churches to explore Christian life. Loving our neighbors as ourselves—the second most important commandment after loving God with all our heart, mind, and strength—is easy for some, but it can be difficult others. We can pray that God opens our hearts and gives us the confidence to invite others into our circle.

Who is God bringing to your attention?

_____

_____

_____

_____

_____

_____

_____

_____

# Day 27

> Do not judge, and you will not be judged. Do no condemn, and you will not be condemned. Forgive and you will be forgiven.
>
> —Luke 6:37

Forgiveness is an intricate and complicated thing. Yet with God's help, forgiveness can be so easy and freeing. Sometimes it's easy to forgive others, but when we look at our own lives and all we wish we had done differently, we can struggle with fully forgiving ourselves and allowing the full view of eternal life before us. Do you view yourself as worthy of saving, of redemption, of eternal life with Jesus? We all fall short of perfection, but through the grace of God and the blood of Jesus Christ, we are saved. All we have to do is ask. Here is one way to ask: "Dear Lord, take my hand, I surrender all of my successes and failures, my hopes and dreams, my life, to You. Father God, lead me on the path of righteousness so that one day I can spend eternity with you. I want to know You, Jesus, and seek a deeper relationship with You, my Lord and Savior. Amen.

What is God saying to you today?

_____

_____

_____

_____

_____

_____

# Day 28

> Anyone who does not provide for their relatives and especially for their own household, has denied the faith and is worse than an unbeliever.
> —1 Timothy 5:8

All generations and all cultures have their own level of what they consider to be "provision" for their children. What is expected today would have been considered very extravagant in the 1940s. It has always been unacceptable to leave a relative who is honestly struggling with illness or unforeseen tragedy without support from family. It has also always been unacceptable to be lazy and not provide for your family.

There are times in every family where a disagreement erupts—and the desire to provide emotional or financial support is depleted. This weakness of the heart is an opportunity to let God step in and heal wounds if you turn this over to Him. When we are weak and allow Him to take over, His light shines the brightest. That is when miracles happen. Surrender any situation you have with a family member to Him, let the love of Jesus wash over you and your loved one, open the door of communication to them, and let the Holy Spirit infuse your words and actions with love. With Jesus in your heart, you can love someone again.

Is there someone in your life who needs this message? How could you present it to them?

_____

_____

_____

# Day 29

> But He would withdraw to desolate places and
> pray.
>
> —Luke 5:16

Being alone has generally negative connotations, but it is a very healthy practice. At the time of the Bible verse, Jesus was publicly teaching and healing people, and there were always crowds around Him. The energy of His human body was being sapped.

In personality tests, they sometimes ask, "Do you get energized by being with people or by being alone?" My husband is one of the most extroverted people I know, but he does need time alone to recharge when no one is talking to him. Blaise Pascal wrote, "All men's miseries derive from not being able to sit quiet in a room alone." Spending time alone is necessary for people to become unique individuals and to deeply develop thoughts, works, and ideas. Always chasing social engagement can have negative consequences. Take time away to give yourself an opportunity to think deeply about your spirituality, relationships, and God-driven inspirations.

How is taking quiet time healthy for both introverts and extroverts?

_____

_____

_____

_____

_____

# Day 30

> Be completely humble and gentle; be patient,
> bearing with one another in love.
>
> —Ephesians 4:2

We recently had a discussion in our family of adult children about who takes longer to get ready to go somewhere outside the home, and overwhelmingly, the women thought the men took longer. The frustration was real! There was laughter involved, of course, because it was not a relationship-breaking issue. However, cumulatively, these frustrations, if not dealt with, can cause relationships to sour. In these situations, we need to check ourselves or speak with another Christian to get their perspective to determine whether a discussion is warranted. Then we can humbly and gently talk about how we are feeling and—bearing with one another—come up with compromises that work for both people.

We are not going to change a calm, even-keeled person into a driven, fast-paced person or vice versa. That is not how God created that person to be. We have to get back to what attracted us to the person in the first place. Maybe God gave you that relationship to help you come to the middle. On the flip side, if you are receiving the constructive criticism, realize that if the person is taking the time and energy to tell you their concerns, you mean enough to them to spend their energy on you. You are worth their time to figure out a solution. This is love—even though it may not feel like it is at the time. Pray together for solutions, and God will bless your relationship.

Is there resentment building in a relationship that you need to give to God?

_____

_____

# Day 32

> Do you not know that your bodies are temples of
> the Holy Spirit, who is in you, whom you have
> received from God? You are not your own.
> —1 Corinthians 6:19

When you think about the human body and how complex every part of it is, there is no denying our divine creation. Every one of us is beautiful and unique. Every one of us has special talents. Taking care of our bodies is a challenging thing because there are so many temptations and choices throughout the day. When you surrender your body to a higher power, you get nudged in the right direction, but the decisions are always yours. Do you ever feel like time stands still when you are making a choice on a menu, selecting food at a grocery store, or deciding who to hang out with or whether or not to exercise? This is possibly a way for the Holy Spirit to nudge us in the right direction. Things like alcohol, the media, and other people can sidetrack us. It is good to celebrate and indulge occasionally, but if you see a pattern of overindulgence or the inability to make good decisions, consider making a plan that will lead you on a healthier path. Your body is a temple of the Holy Spirit, beautiful and clean.

What pattern in your life do you see a need for change?

_____

_____

_____

_____

_____

# Day 33

> I keep asking that the God of our Lord Jesus
> Christ, the glorious Father, may give you the
> Spirit of wisdom and revelation, so that you may
> know Him better.
>
> —Ephesians 1:17

At the time Ephesians was written, Paul was going around
Ephesus preaching the good news to Jews and Gentiles and
sparking a new church to be formed with Jesus's teachings as
the center. This new life with Christ emphasized forgiveness,
love, hope, and grace for everyone. With this new life came a
relationship with a higher power in which you could ask for
wisdom and knowledge. With this wisdom, you have a new way
of looking at and treating other humans. No longer was everyone
in their separate Jews versus non-Jews groups. Everyone was
welcome to the gift of salvation. Everyone was invited to ask
for wisdom and knowledge that would change their lives and
the whole outlook on the world. What a revelation for this
community! May we have this spirit of sharing the good news
with others.

Is there anyone who needs your prayer that they would be open
to hearing the good news?

_____

_____

_____

_____

_____

# Day 34

> You have made known to me the paths of life;
> you will fill me with joy in your presence.
>
> —Acts 2:28

When I read this verse and let it sink into my being, I am given a feeling of joy that cannot be replicated with any earthly thing. It is a joy that brings my tense shoulders down, empties my mind of worry, and expands and frees my heart and lungs. I automatically feel my face relaxing and a gently smile forming on my lips. Jesus's presence gives peace and joy to us. This is a gift that all you have to give is your time and invitation for Him to come into your space. It's pure love and gentleness. Divine love is hard to describe, but in human terms, it might be the warm smell of a pie baking combined with the view of a mountain in the morning mist and topped with the first moments of holding your newborn baby. These moments do not come without practicing spending time with God and developing the skills of quieting the mind and body. His presence will be made known to you, and He will fill you with joy.

How can you follow the path of life, leading to joy?

_____

_____

_____

_____

_____

_____

# Day 35

> But the fruit of the Spirit is love, joy, peace,
> forbearance, kindness, goodness, faithfulness,
> gentleness, and self-control. Against such things
> there is no law.
>
> —Galatians 5:22–23

If I ever got a tattoo, I think it would be this verse because it's all
the character assets that I feel are important in life. I fall short
every day, but at least I would have them on my outside! It's
important to have an attitude of striving to be a good person,
but all of us are human and imperfect. We feel bad when we
do something we know is wrong, but we don't need to dwell
on it. We can ask for forgiveness and then look at ourselves in
a positive way with all the characteristics listed above. Because
we are children of God, we can be made perfect by forgiveness.
Meditating on those character traits and infusing them into our
minds, souls, and bodies helps us take one step closer each day
to being like Jesus.

Which character trait or traits spark an interest for you?

_____

_____

_____

_____

_____

_____

# Day 36

> Whoever believes in me, as scripture has said,
> rivers of living water will flow from within them.
> —John 7:38

Rivers of living water can flow from within you. It is not just a trickle of water; it is rivers of living water! We have more ability and potential to speak the truth and share the Word than we sometimes realize. Rivers of living water could also mean doing good things. Whenever we share our talents to help someone else, it is letting Jesus's love flow.

We belong to a small group; we call it House Church. Once a month, we try to do a service project, such as helping an elderly person with home repairs, helping a person who is sick have an accessible deck, or landscaping the church. Anything that goes beyond ourselves helps us let love flow from us. We have been the recipients of this time as well. When we moved, our House Church family helped us. It was incredible to receive this act of love, which our culture typically shuns, because we are expected to be independent. It was good for us to be on the receiving end of this in order to experience the love going into us like a battery recharge. It overflowed to the point that I shed tears of gratitude. Do not be afraid to let rivers of living water run through your life by giving and receiving.

How can you let the rivers of living water run in and out of your life?

_____

_____

_____

# Day 37

> Your Word is a lamp for my feet, a light on my path.
>
> —Psalm 119:105

Studying God's work and embedding it into your heart gives you insight into the world that is beyond human understanding. Picture standing in an unfamiliar dark room that you need to cross. You could probably get through that room by stumbling and bumping your way through, groping around to find your way. You are thinking, *A light would really help right now.*

Life presents problems that we are unfamiliar with, and we often rush through without thinking about the best tool to use in that situation. In your life, you *do* have a tool available to light your path. Now picture the same dark room and a flashlight in your hand; that is the Bible, scripture, God's Word. You turn it on, and you can see that path and take the first step.

Every question and obstacle in life can be answered—or at least the general direction can be found in it. It is a guide for life. As you continually read it, different parts stand out with meaning for your life. Many times, I have read a passage that sounds new because I don't remember having read it. It is always fresh and new because our lives change. We need different parts of the Bible to shine a light on our path. Keep this flashlight in your hand, heart, and mind at all times. We have a choice to walk in light or darkness, stumbling, groping, and falling or following a lighted path. God's Word is a lamp unto our feet and our path ahead.

How can God's Word be a light for you?

_____

_____

# Day 38

> You will keep in perfect peace those, whose minds are steadfast because they trust in you.
>
> —Isaiah 26:3

Francis de Sales said, "Half an hour's meditation is essential except when you are very busy. Then a full hour is needed." That quote is quite humorous because it contradicts the natural tendency to cut back on something to make up time. Doesn't it seem like we are always looking for more time? We can look at this differently by recognizing when we are stressed or have a tight schedule. Give it to God, and He will be with you all day. He will give us peace when we put our trust in Him. Our time is really His time, and we need to remember that He is in control.

If you run around all stressed out, what does this get you? People around you take on your stress, and the culture of your home or work environment can turn negative or even toxic. God wants His people to be remembered as kind, peaceful, and loving. There are people who will attempt to distract and pull you away from this time with God, albeit inadvertently. But remember, all time is God's, and if we keep our minds focused on Him and trust in Him to guide us through each day, we will have that peace beyond human ability.

How can you show peacefulness and kindness today?

_____

_____

_____

_____

_____

## Day 39

> Let us not become weary in doing good, for at
> the proper time we will reap a harvest if we do
> not give up.
>
> —Galatians 6:9

Sometimes things take longer than we expect. For example, you may pray about something, and there doesn't seem to be an answer. You might be working on a project that seems to drag on forever without any fruit. If you give it to God, pray about it, and ask others to pray for you too, you will eventually see a harvest.

Many times, I have seen God teaching us patience and persistence when we would prefer to see the results *now*. This waiting and working teaches us self-discipline and delayed gratification, which are very important traits for a stable person. To be the best person you can be, you cannot expect everything to be handed to you whenever you ask because you would become like a spoiled child. No one would want to be around you. These are very hard lessons to learn, but in retrospect, you will have the wisdom to use for the future. You can help others who are growing weary of doing good, waiting for prayers to be answered, and thinking about giving up.

How can waiting a long time for something be a good thing?

_____

_____

_____

_____

_____

# Day 40

> Do not judge and you will not be judged. Do not condemn, and you will not be condemned. Forgive and you will be forgiven. Give and it will be given to you. A good measure, pressed down, shaken together and running over, will be poured into your lap. For with the measure you use, it will be measured to you.
>
> —Luke 5:37–38

If we want to know how God perceives us, all we have to do is look at how we treat our neighbors. Do we take the time to let them know we care—or do we ignore them or treat them with contempt? We could stay tucked away in our comfy houses, hoping to not be bothered. Might that be our inheritance then that our Father would ignore our needs? That may sound rather harsh, but it is something to consider. Let's make sure that we are not slowly slipping into our comfort zones, looking out for ourselves, and hoarding our gifts. Giving should come from the heart without expecting anything in return. Whenever you give your time, your talents, your things, or your money, blessings come back to you multiplied. With a kind and generous life, kindness and generosity will come flooding back to you in full measure.

How can we be good examples of this verse in our life?

_____

_____

_____

_____

## Bible Challenge

Here is a forty-day scripture verse challenge. The purpose is to learn to open the Bible, find the verse, and read the verse and the surrounding chapter or book. This will help you become more comfortable opening the Bible—and you can choose how much to read. Reading the chapter around the verse can give you more insight about the meaning and context. Write the verse down, repeat the verse, and meditate on it. Then journal using the question or what God speaks into your life.

Day 1: Revelation 17:14

What situation in your life do you need to give to God?

_____

_____

_____

_____

_____

_____

_____

_____

_____

_____

_____

_____

_____

Day 2: Philippians 2:13

What goal or dream is God putting on your heart?

_____

_____

_____

_____

_____

_____

_____

_____

_____

_____

_____

_____

_____

_____

Day 3: Ephesians 4:30

What thought, word, or deed do you need forgiveness for?

_____

_____

_____

_____

_____

_____

_____

_____

_____

_____

_____

_____

_____

Day 4: Psalm 118:24

What do you need to celebrate with God about?

_____

_____

_____

_____

_____

_____

_____

_____

_____

_____

_____

_____

_____

Day 5: Psalm 100:4

What are you thankful for?

_____

_____

_____

_____

_____

_____

_____

_____

_____

_____

_____

_____

_____

Day 6: Deuteronomy 33:12

How is God telling you he loves you?

_____

_____

_____

_____

_____

_____

_____

_____

_____

_____

_____

_____

_____

Day 7: Philippians 4:5–6

How is God using you to do things you would be able to do on your own?

_____

_____

_____

_____

_____

_____

_____

_____

_____

_____

_____

_____

_____

_____

Day 8: John 8:32

What worry, anxiety, or stress can God help you with today?

_____

_____

_____

_____

_____

_____

_____

_____

_____

_____

_____

_____

_____

_____

Day 9: Ephesians 6:16

What action does God want you to take today?

_____

_____

_____

_____

_____

_____

_____

_____

_____

_____

_____

_____

_____

_____

Day 10: Psalm 48:9

What is God saying to you in this moment?

_____

_____

_____

_____

_____

_____

_____

_____

_____

_____

_____

_____

_____

_____

Day 11: Ephesians 5:8

Who is God bringing to your attention?

_____

_____

_____

_____

_____

_____

_____

_____

_____

_____

_____

_____

_____

Day 12: Psalm 91:1

What situation in your life do you need to give to God?

_____

_____

_____

_____

_____

_____

_____

_____

_____

_____

_____

_____

_____

_____

Day 13: Philippians 2:15

What thought, word, or deed do you need forgiveness for?

_____

_____

_____

_____

_____

_____

_____

_____

_____

_____

_____

_____

_____

_____

Day 14: Psalm 95:1–2

What victory do you need to celebrate with God about?

_____

_____

_____

_____

_____

_____

_____

_____

_____

_____

_____

_____

_____

_____

Day 15: Psalm 100:4

What are you thankful for?

_____

_____

_____

_____

_____

_____

_____

_____

_____

_____

_____

_____

_____

_____

Day 16: Luke 1:79

Who is God bringing to your attention?

_____

_____

_____

_____

_____

_____

_____

_____

_____

_____

_____

_____

_____

Day 17: Psalm 34:5

How is God telling you He loves you?

_____

_____

_____

_____

_____

_____

_____

_____

_____

_____

_____

_____

_____

_____

Day 18: 2 Corinthians 4:16–17

What worry, anxiety, or stress can God help you with today?

_____

_____

_____

_____

_____

_____

_____

_____

_____

_____

_____

_____

_____

_____

Day 19: Psalm 42:1–2

What action does God want you to take today?

_____

_____

_____

_____

_____

_____

_____

_____

_____

_____

_____

_____

_____

_____

Day 20: Isaiah 55:8–9

What is God saying to you in this moment?

_____

_____

_____

_____

_____

_____

_____

_____

_____

_____

_____

_____

_____

Day 21: Proverbs 3:5

What situation in your life do you need to give to God?

_____

_____

_____

_____

_____

_____

_____

_____

_____

_____

_____

_____

_____

Day 22: Psalm 42:1–2

What action does God want you to take today?

_____

_____

_____

_____

_____

_____

_____

_____

_____

_____

_____

_____

_____

Day 23: Isaiah 12:2

Who is God bringing to your attention?

_____

_____

_____

_____

_____

_____

_____

_____

_____

_____

_____

_____

_____

Day 24: 2 Corinthians 12:9

What goal or dream is God putting on your heart?

_____

_____

_____

_____

_____

_____

_____

_____

_____

_____

_____

_____

_____

_____

Day 25: Ephesians 5:8–10

What thought, word, or deed do you need forgiveness for?

_____

_____

_____

_____

_____

_____

_____

_____

_____

_____

_____

_____

_____

Day 26: Philippians 4:4–5

What victory do you need to celebrate with God about?

_____

_____

_____

_____

_____

_____

_____

_____

_____

_____

_____

_____

_____

_____

Day 27: Psalm 28:7

What are you thankful for?

_____

_____

_____

_____

_____

_____

_____

_____

_____

_____

_____

_____

_____

_____

Day 28: Zephaniah 3:17

How is God telling you He loves you?

_____

_____

_____

_____

_____

_____

_____

_____

_____

_____

_____

_____

_____

_____

Day 29: Psalm 34:5

What is God saying to you in this moment?

_____

_____

_____

_____

_____

_____

_____

_____

_____

_____

_____

_____

_____

_____

Day 30: Ephesians 6:16

What action does God want you to take today?

_____

_____

_____

_____

_____

_____

_____

_____

_____

_____

_____

_____

_____

Day 31: Philippians 2:15

Who is God brining to your attention?

_____

_____

_____

_____

_____

_____

_____

_____

_____

_____

_____

_____

_____

Day 32: Isaiah 31:15

What situation in your life do you need to give to God?

_____

_____

_____

_____

_____

_____

_____

_____

_____

_____

_____

_____

_____

_____

Day 33: Psalm 31:14

What goal or dream is God putting on your heart?

_____

_____

_____

_____

_____

_____

_____

_____

_____

_____

_____

_____

_____

Day 34: 1 John 1:5–7

What thought, word, or deed do you need forgiveness for?

_____

_____

_____

_____

_____

_____

_____

_____

_____

_____

_____

_____

_____

_____

Day 35: Romans 12:12

What do you need to celebrate with God about?

_____

_____

_____

_____

_____

_____

_____

_____

_____

_____

_____

_____

_____

_____

Day 36: Thessalonians 5:18

What are you thankful for?

_____

_____

_____

_____

_____

_____

_____

_____

_____

_____

_____

_____

_____

Day 37: Song of Songs 2:13

How is God telling you He loves you?

_____

_____

_____

_____

_____

_____

_____

_____

_____

_____

_____

_____

_____

_____

Day 38: Psalm 119:35

How is God using you to do things you wouldn't be able to do on your own?

_____

_____

_____

_____

_____

_____

_____

_____

_____

_____

_____

_____

_____

_____

Day 39: Isaiah 12:2

What worry, anxiety, or stress can God help you with today?

_____

_____

_____

_____

_____

_____

_____

_____

_____

_____

_____

_____

Day 40: Isaiah 30:15

What is God saying to you in this moment?

_____

_____

_____

_____

_____

_____

_____

_____

_____

_____

_____

_____

_____

Now that you have tried different ways of spending time with God, you may find that you prefer one way over another. I hope you have established a new routine in your life that will last forever. May the hope and peace of Jesus be in your heart and be shared with all around you!

# Acknowledgements

This book was such a labor of love that God put on my heart—so all praise and glory go to Him, who gave me the words to share with you. There is no doubt in my mind that this is His work as the words seemed to just flow out like a stream.

Eric, my husband, you are the best teammate I could ever ask for. You are always supporting me when God puts a mission on my heart, giving Godly wisdom and discernment. You help me have the confidence to continue working His plan.

Alison Olson, you read through this book more than once, gave me such great advice, and gave me encouragement to keep going; it is ever appreciated.

Sonja Knutson, what can I say? You are my mentor, leader, and someone I look up to for guidance. You are always speaking empowerment and courage into my life when I start doubting my calling.

My daughters and Journey group friends, you helped me determine that this book was needed. When I came to you with the idea, you had words of affirmation that helped steer me forward. You've been praying me through the whole process, and I am so thankful for all of you!

And finally, to the Westbow Press team, thank you for walking me through this process.

# About the Author

**Tamera Thoreson** is a Christian author who has been involved in her church and many mission projects and trips both locally and globally. She and her husband have four grown children and two grandchildren and live in Minnesota.